History of The Persian Empire

CRAFTED BY SKRIUWER

Copyright © 2025 by Skriuwer.

All rights reserved. No part of this book may be used or reproduced in any form whatsoever without written permission except in the case of brief quotations in critical articles or reviews.

At **Skriuwer**, we're more than just a team—we're a global community of people who love books. In Frisian, "Skriuwer" means "writer," and that's at the heart of what we do: creating and sharing books with readers worldwide. Wherever you are in the world, **Skriuwer** is here to inspire learning.

Frisian is one of the oldest languages in Europe, closely related to English and Dutch, and is spoken by about **500,000 people** in the province of **Friesland** (Fryslân), located in the northern Netherlands. It's the second official language of the Netherlands, but like many minority languages, Frisian faces the challenge of survival in a modern, globalized world.

We're using the money we earn to promote the Frisian language.

For more information, contact : **kontakt@skriuwer.com** (www.skriuwer.com)

Disclaimer:
The images in this book are creative reinterpretations of historical scenes. While every effort was made to accurately capture the essence of the periods depicted, some illustrations may include artistic embellishments or approximations. They are intended to evoke the atmosphere and spirit of the times rather than serve as precise historical records.

TABLE OF CONTENTS

CHAPTER 1: THE LAND BEFORE THE KINGS

- Early tribal life on the Iranian Plateau
- Influence of the Elamites and Medes
- Foundations of future Persian culture

CHAPTER 2: THE RISE OF THE ACHAEMENID DYNASTY

- Origins of the House of Achaemenes
- Persian alliances with the Medes
- Steps toward unification and early conquests

CHAPTER 3: CYRUS THE GREAT

- Rebellion against the Medes and Astyages
- Expansion into Lydia and Babylon
- Policies of respect and local autonomy

CHAPTER 4: CAMBYSES II AND THE EARLY EXPANSION

- Conquest of Egypt and its impact
- Handling revolts and unrest back home
- Mysterious circumstances of Cambyses's death

CHAPTER 5: DARIUS I AND HIS ADMINISTRATIVE REFORMS

- Satrapy system and the Royal Road
- Standardized coinage and taxation
- Legal codes and monumental building projects

CHAPTER 6: XERXES I AND THE WARS WITH GREECE

- Thermopylae, Salamis, and Greek resistance
- Strategic withdrawals and palace intrigues
- Aftermath of the failed western campaign

CHAPTER 7: LATER ACHAEMENID RULERS AND THE FALL OF THE EMPIRE

- Succession issues and internal struggles
- Weakening control over far-flung provinces
- Vulnerability to external threats

CHAPTER 8: ALEXANDER THE GREAT AND THE END OF ACHAEMENID RULE

- Rapid conquest of Persia
- Destruction of Persepolis
- Blending Greek and Persian cultures

CHAPTER 9: THE SELEUCID PERIOD

- Struggle to maintain a Hellenistic empire
- Foundation of Greek-style cities in Iran
- Rise of local forces like Bactria and Parthia

CHAPTER 10: THE RISE OF THE PARTHIAN EMPIRE

- Arsaces and the overthrow of Seleucid governors
- Cavalry innovations and early Parthian conquests
- Establishing a loose confederation of nobles

CHAPTER 11: THE HEIGHT OF PARTHIAN POWER

- *Economic prosperity and Silk Road trade*
- *Diplomatic ties and conflicts with Rome*
- *Refinement of Parthian culture and noble structures*

CHAPTER 12: CONFLICTS WITH ROME AND THE DECLINE OF PARTHIA

- *Repeated clashes over Mesopotamia*
- *Internal divisions and weak central authority*
- *Path set for Sasanian takeover*

CHAPTER 13: THE FALL OF THE PARTHIAN EMPIRE

- *Sasanian revolt led by Ardashir I*
- *Battle of Hormizdegan and defeat of Artabanus IV*
- *Transition to a new Persian dynasty*

CHAPTER 14: THE BEGINNING OF THE SASANIAN EMPIRE

- *Ardashir I's consolidation of power*
- *Linking monarchy with Zoroastrianism*
- *Revival of Persian art and administration*

CHAPTER 15: SHAPUR I AND THE EARLY SASANIAN STRENGTH

- *Wars with Rome and the capture of Valerian*
- *Use of skilled prisoners in building projects*
- *Cultural and religious developments*

CHAPTER 16: THE GOLDEN AGE OF THE SASANIAN EMPIRE

- Economic growth and flourishing trade routes
- Artistic achievements and strong central governance
- Managing religious diversity and growing orthodoxy

CHAPTER 17: WARS WITH ROME AND BYZANTIUM

- Cycles of conflict and precarious truces
- Military innovations in cavalry and siege warfare
- Diplomatic marriages and shifting alliances

CHAPTER 18: THE LATER SASANIAN RULERS

- Succession disputes and noble rivalries
- Reforms under Kavad I and Khosrow I
- Pressure from nomadic forces in the east

CHAPTER 19: THE FALL OF THE SASANIAN EMPIRE

- Aftermath of Khosrow II's defeat
- Arab conquests and battles like Qadisiyyah
- End of Yazdegerd III's reign and collapse of the monarchy

CHAPTER 20: THE LEGACY OF ANCIENT PERSIA

- Administrative heritage and cultural imprint
- Influence on art, religion, and kingship
- Persian identity evolving into the Islamic era

CHAPTER 1

THE LAND BEFORE THE KINGS

Introduction

In this first chapter, we will step back into a time before any famous Persian kings existed. We will look at the early environment, the climate, and the people who lived on the Iranian Plateau. We will also see the kinds of customs and beliefs that shaped these early communities. This will help us understand how the land itself influenced the rise of the Persian Empire.

Geography and Climate of the Iranian Plateau

The Iranian Plateau is a big piece of land. It stretches from the mountains in the northwest to deserts in the east and southeast. The region has high, rugged mountains and wide, dry plains. There are also some rivers that bring life to the land, although they are not as large as rivers like the Nile or the Tigris. People who lived here had to adapt to different kinds of environments. Some places had enough water for farming, but many areas were very dry.

Life was not easy, and the changing seasons made it even harder. In the winter, some parts of the plateau get snow, while the southern areas stay warmer. In the summer, many places become very hot and dry. Early communities had to figure out ways to survive, such as digging wells for water, building canals, or learning to herd animals that did not need a lot of water.

The First Inhabitants

Before great rulers like Cyrus or Darius, there were tribes and small villages scattered across the plateau. Many of these people were hunters and gatherers at first. They roamed the land in search of game and edible plants. Over time, they learned how to farm crops like wheat and barley. They also started to domesticate animals such as sheep, goats, and cattle.

As these small groups began to farm, they stayed in one place for longer periods. Villages turned into small towns, and people began to build permanent homes from mud bricks or stones. This started a new way of life. Instead of moving around all the time, they created settlements where they lived year-round.

They developed simple forms of government too. Often, a chief or an elder led the group. The elders made decisions about sharing water, dividing farmland, and protecting the community. These little settlements also practiced simple crafts, like pottery and weaving. They made pots to store food and water, and they made cloth from wool to keep warm in the colder months.

Early Beliefs and Customs

We do not know all the details about how these early people worshipped or what gods they might have prayed to. But from the remains of their pottery and small statues, we can guess that they believed in some form of higher power. Many early societies built small altars or used open-air places for worship. They might have prayed for good harvests or for help in finding water.

Stories and myths were important too. They passed these stories down from parents to children. These tales explained natural events like thunderstorms, droughts, or floods. Because they did not have scientific knowledge, they often saw these events as signs from the gods or spirits. Over time, such beliefs shaped the future religions of the area, including the ideas that later became part of Zoroastrianism.

The Significance of Trade

The land was not just home to separate villages. People from different areas began to trade with each other. Some settlements had good farmland, so they grew wheat and barley. Others lived near mountains with deposits of metal ores like copper or tin. Still others were near trade routes that led to distant lands.

Trade brought new ideas, technology, and even beliefs to these villages. People learned different ways to shape metal tools or weapons. They exchanged goods like textiles, spices, and precious stones. Over time, bigger market towns grew, where traders met and sold their goods. Trade also connected the plateau to neighboring regions, such as Mesopotamia and Central Asia.

The Elamites and Their Influence

Before the rise of the famous Persian Empire, one of the major early groups in this region was the Elamites. Their main center was in a place called Elam, located in the southwestern area of modern Iran. They had their own language and their own way of writing. While they are not the same as the later Persian kings, they played a big role in shaping the land that would become part of the Persian Empire.

Elam was close to Mesopotamia, which means they were in contact with the Sumerians and Akkadians. They learned from these neighboring cultures, and they sometimes fought them too. Over many centuries, the Elamites built cities, developed trade networks, and created artwork that showed their own style. They also had kings and a structure of government. Their ideas about how to rule and how to organize an army might have influenced later Persian rulers.

The Medes and the Road to Unification

Another important group that lived in the north and northwest part of the plateau were the Medes. The Medes are believed to have come from tribes that spoke an Indo-European language. They arrived in the region around the same time as other related groups who would later call themselves Persians. Over time, the Medes grew stronger and started to form their own state.

We do not know a lot about the Medes because they did not leave many written records of their own. Much of what we know comes from later accounts, including those from the Persians and even from the Greeks. But it seems clear that the Medes built a kingdom that stretched across a big part of the plateau. They controlled trade routes and farmland. They also created alliances with neighboring tribes. This set the stage for bigger things to come, because once tribes got used to forming alliances, they learned how to unite under one ruler.

Daily Life in Early Times

Although we do not have detailed texts describing everyday life, we can guess that most people in these early centuries were farmers or herders. They woke up early to tend to their fields or their animals. They lived in houses made of mud bricks, with flat roofs. Family life was very important, and many households included not just parents and children but also grandparents, aunts, uncles, and cousins.

Women worked at home and in the fields too. They raised children and made clothing. Men often took care of heavier tasks like plowing or building. People used simple tools, such as stone or copper knives, wooden plows, and clay pottery for storing water or food. Communities were close-knit, and neighbors helped each other with big tasks like harvesting or building homes.

Early Art and Crafts

Even in these simple times, art was part of daily life. People decorated their pottery with lines, circles, or images of animals. Sometimes they carved small figures out of stone or wood. Craftsmen learned how to work with metals to make jewelry, tools, and small statues. Over time, they got better at shaping bronze, which is made by mixing copper with tin. This allowed them to create stronger tools and nicer ornaments.

Music and dance were likely a part of village festivals. When the harvest was good, communities might gather to share food, play instruments, and dance. Though we do not have recordings from that time, we have found old instruments like simple flutes or drums in some archaeological sites. This shows that people valued joy and celebration even in harsh environments.

Growth of Early Towns and Cities

As trade grew, some settlements became bigger. They turned into towns with markets, workshops, and temples. These towns needed organization, so local chiefs or councils managed resources and settled disputes. Over time, the idea of a single ruler in charge of a larger area began to form. The land needed protection from raiders, and strong leaders who could unite various tribes became more popular.

When these small states and towns became connected, the idea of having one king for many groups no longer seemed strange. The Medes were one of the first to try this, and they brought several smaller tribes under their control. This was an important step on the path to the grand Persian Empire that would appear later.

The Role of Horses

Horses played a crucial role in the ancient Near East. As people learned to ride horses or use them to pull carts and chariots, travel and warfare changed. Horses could move faster than donkeys or oxen. This meant news, goods, and armies could travel across the plateau more quickly.

Some early communities became skilled horse breeders. They traded horses with neighboring lands. Horses also became symbols of status, especially for warriors and the chiefs. In many tales, a leader's skill in riding horses or driving a chariot showed power and greatness. Later, Persian armies would use horse-riding warriors who were famous for their skill in battle.

The Formation of Customs and Culture

Even though many different tribes lived in the region, they shared some common customs over time. For example, hospitality was very important. If a traveler came to a village, it was polite to give them food and shelter. This tradition continued throughout Persian history and can still be seen in some parts of the region today, although we are not going to focus on modern times.

Another custom that grew among these tribes was respect for elders. People believed that older members of the community had wisdom. They had seen many seasons of drought and plenty, so they knew how to survive in tough times. This respect for elders later appeared in Persian writings and stories about kings who listened to wise counselors.

Early Conflicts and Alliances

Life was not always peaceful. Tribes sometimes fought over land or water sources. A shortage of water in a dry region can lead to conflicts. Some groups wanted to take over places with wells or rivers so they could farm better. Other groups preferred to herd animals, which required open grazing land. Disagreements could lead to battles, and winners would claim new territories.

But just as often, tribes formed alliances to protect each other from outside threats. The arrival of new groups from the north or east forced local tribes to work together. They agreed to help each other if raiders attacked. Over time, these alliances became more structured, leading to the idea of a kingdom with a single ruler. The Medes are a good example of this process. They took many smaller tribes under their wing, sometimes by force, sometimes by offering protection.

Language and Early Writing

We do not have many written records from the earliest periods, but we do know that multiple languages were spoken. Some were local, while others belonged to newcomers. Over time, these languages mixed. Simple writing systems began to appear, influenced by Mesopotamia. Clay tablets and cylinder seals were used to record trade deals or mark ownership.

The Elamites had their own writing system, which they used for administrative records. This writing system helps us see how advanced their government structure was. Later on, as the Persians came to power, they developed cuneiform inscriptions in Old Persian for their royal declarations, influenced in part by these earlier scripts.

Religion and the Roots of Zoroastrian Ideas

While true Zoroastrianism likely emerged later, some of its seeds may have been planted during this time. Many tribes believed in spirits of nature, like sky gods or fire gods. Fire was seen as very important because it gave warmth and light. People also looked at the sun as a powerful force. Over time, these ideas shaped the religious beliefs that would be common in Persia.

Many scholars think that some of the early Iranian-speaking tribes carried beliefs that later became part of Zoroastrianism. This faith, as we will see in later chapters, taught about the fight between good and evil, truth and lies. But in these early days, it was just forming. People were more concerned with everyday survival than with deep religious teachings.

Contacts with Other Civilizations

The Iranian Plateau did not stand alone. There were connections with places like Mesopotamia, the Indus Valley, and even distant lands like the steppes of Central Asia. Traders passed through with goods, and sometimes people moved from one region to another. This movement brought new ideas, such as metalworking or ways of building stronger walls.

In times of peace, these contacts allowed for cultural exchange. Craftsmen learned new designs. Farmers tried new crops. Rulers heard about different governing methods. In times of war, these contacts meant raids or invasions. Armies from the west, such as the Assyrians, sometimes marched east and clashed with tribes on the plateau. Such conflicts taught local peoples the need for stronger defenses and better organization.

Preparing the Stage for the Achaemenids

The story of the Persian Empire truly begins with the rise of the Achaemenid Dynasty. But we cannot jump there without seeing how these early tribes, especially the Medes, laid the foundation. By the time of the 7th century BCE, the Medes had formed a kingdom that included many smaller groups. Some of these groups were Persian tribes who lived more to the south, near a region called Parsa (or Fars in some later languages).

As we move into the next chapters, we will see how a Persian family (the Achaemenids) came to power. They built on the work of the Medes and also drew lessons from the Elamites. They formed what would become one of the largest empires in the ancient world. But at this point in the story, all of that is still in the future. The land is a collection of tribes, small kingdoms, and budding cities, each with its own leaders and customs.

Challenges Faced by Early Rulers

Even though we talk of kings and chiefs, we should remember that no single king ruled all of the plateau in these early times. Leaders faced many problems. They had to keep people from fighting each other. They had to gather resources for building and for feeding their people. Travel was slow, and sending messages across large distances took time.

Moreover, nature was a big challenge. Periods of drought could ruin harvests, causing famines. Storms or floods in some areas could destroy homes and fields. Disease could spread if the water supply was not clean. Early rulers had to make sure that essential tasks—like digging canals and storing water—were done properly. If they failed, people might starve, or the community might break apart and follow another leader.

The Blend of Cultures

It is important to realize that the Iranian Plateau was home to a mix of peoples. This blend made the region rich in ideas. Pottery styles, clothing, even ways of worship varied. Some groups wore simple tunics, while others might have had more elaborate robes. Some groups buried their dead with grave goods, while others practiced different burial customs.

Over time, these differences began to form a broader culture that shared some core ideas but still had local flavors. This blend would later help the Persian Empire, because it showed that people in this land were used to diversity. When the Achaemenids came to power, they also respected the customs of different peoples, which helped them rule a large territory.

Key Transitions

The step from small communities to large kingdoms was slow. It involved many trials, alliances, and even betrayals. Some chiefs might declare themselves kings, only to lose power later. Others learned to be diplomatic, forging ties through marriages or gifts. Cattle, horses, and precious items could be offered to a neighboring tribe to keep the peace.

Eventually, a new idea took shape: the idea that one king could rule many lands by setting up local governors or letting local chiefs keep their authority if they swore loyalty. This was not yet the advanced system we see under Darius I, but it was an early version of how to manage a big territory. The Medes are credited by some historians with using this method, and the Persians improved it.

CHAPTER 2

THE RISE OF THE ACHAEMENID DYNASTY

Introduction

In the last chapter, we learned about the land and the different tribes that lived on the Iranian Plateau before the famous Persian kings. We saw how groups like the Medes and the Elamites created the groundwork for bigger kingdoms. Now, we will focus on the rise of the Achaemenid Dynasty. This dynasty started small but grew into a major power that challenged even the strongest forces of the ancient world.

Who Were the Achaemenids?

The Achaemenids were a royal family line that claimed to be descendants of a man named Achaemenes. We do not have much direct evidence about Achaemenes himself. Later Persian kings wrote about him as the founder of their house. Whether he was a real person or partly a legend, he became an important symbol.

The early Achaemenids controlled a region called Parsa (later known as Fars). At first, they were just one of many tribes in the area. But they had close ties to the Medes, who were very powerful at that time. By forming alliances and marriages, the Achaemenids grew in influence. They also learned from the Medes about how to organize and govern lands.

The Role of Teispes, Cyrus I, and Cambyses I

Several names appear in early Achaemenid history, such as Teispes, Cyrus I, and Cambyses I. These rulers are said to have led the

Persians before the famous Cyrus II, often called Cyrus the Great. They might not have ruled large empires, but they held their own territories. Their control might have been limited to certain districts in Parsa and nearby regions.

These early kings did important work by keeping good relations with the Medes. They also protected their people from other enemies like the Elamites or tribes from the east. Over time, they established the idea that the House of Achaemenes had a right to rule. This set the stage for when a stronger leader would finally unite all the Persians under one banner.

The World Around Them

To understand why the Achaemenids rose to power, we should look at what was happening in neighboring lands around the 7th and early 6th centuries BCE. In Mesopotamia, the Assyrian Empire was collapsing. This empire had once been very powerful, but now it was weakening due to revolts and attacks from different sides.

The Medes played a big role in defeating the Assyrians. They joined forces with the Babylonians to capture the Assyrian capital of Nineveh in 612 BCE. After this victory, the Medes became strong in the east, and the Babylonians became strong in the south. For a while, the Medes held sway over the Persians, but this balance of power was about to change.

The Persian-Median Relationship

The Medes had formed their own kingdom, and their king, Astyages, was one of the most powerful rulers in the region. The Persians, under Cambyses I (Cyrus the Great's father), were likely vassals or allies to Astyages. This means they recognized the power of the Median king and probably paid tribute or provided troops.

However, the Persians were also proud and capable. They did not like being completely under the Medes. Historians debate how the famous conflict began, but most agree that Cyrus II (Cyrus the Great) eventually rebelled against his Median overlord. We will learn more about that in Chapter 3. For now, it is enough to say that the groundwork for that rebellion was laid by earlier Achaemenid leaders who kept the Persians united.

Early Military Strength

One reason the Achaemenids could challenge the Medes was because they developed a good military system. The Persians were skilled horsemen and archers. They learned many of these skills from their neighbors, but they also practiced them daily because life on the plateau often involved protecting livestock and fighting off raids.

The idea of an organized army was still growing, but the Persians knew how to form groups of foot soldiers and horse riders. They used bows, spears, and short swords. Their armor was made of leather or metal scales. Leaders who knew how to motivate and coordinate these fighters could become very powerful. This would be a lesson Cyrus the Great would use to his advantage.

Local Governance

Even before they had a huge empire, the Achaemenids learned to manage their territory well. They set up local governors or officials in different areas. These officials were often trusted nobles or relatives of the king. They collected taxes, settled disputes, and kept an eye on trade routes.

Because of the tough environment, ensuring water supply and building roads were big concerns. The Achaemenids understood that if farmers could not get water, they would move away. Also, if roads were unsafe, traders would avoid the region. By maintaining order, the early Achaemenid rulers built trust among the people. When Cyrus the Great later called on them to fight against Astyages, many Persians felt loyal to him.

Cultural and Religious Factors

The Persians, like many peoples in the region, held spiritual beliefs that gave meaning to their lives. We do not know the exact details of their religion at this early stage, but it likely included respect for natural elements like fire and water. Some scholars say these beliefs were an early form of what later became Zoroastrianism.

Cultural unity was also important. The Persian language, customs, and shared stories helped bind the people together. They told tales of heroes, such as great warriors or wise leaders. These stories inspired the young and gave them pride in being Persian. When a strong leader emerged, he could use these shared traditions to unite the various tribes under one cause.

Emerging Power Structures

By the time Cyrus II was born around 600 BCE (the exact date is debated), the Achaemenid house had already formed a decent power base. They might not have been equal to the Medes yet, but they were strong enough to dream of independence.

The downfall of the Assyrian Empire and the rise of new powers like Lydia in the west also changed the political map. In times of great change, brave or ambitious leaders often see opportunities to grow. It was in this environment that Cyrus II would soon emerge as a key figure.

Ties to the Medes Through Marriage

Marriages between royal families were common ways to seal alliances. The Achaemenids likely arranged marriages with noble Median families. Some sources, although they might be legendary, claim that Cyrus II had familial ties to Astyages. This would mean that the war between them was also a conflict within a larger family.

Whether these stories are fully true or not, it is clear that the Achaemenids were not strangers to the Median court. They understood how the Medes governed, how they fought, and how they negotiated treaties. This inside knowledge gave them an edge when Cyrus II decided to oppose Median rule.

Preparations for Expansion

Even before Cyrus II made his move, the Achaemenids were preparing for expansion. They improved their military by training horsemen and archers. They might have also started building or improving fortifications near important towns. Keeping roads and trade routes safe brought in wealth, which they could use to pay for more troops.

These actions show that they were not just a small tribe anymore. They were thinking ahead, looking for ways to increase their influence. Local governors who proved themselves might be given more responsibility. Soldiers who showed bravery might be rewarded with land or riches. Step by step, the foundation for a larger state was being laid.

The Importance of Diplomacy

The Achaemenids did not rely only on force. They also knew how to talk to neighbors in a friendly way. They used gifts and respectful visits to keep peace when needed. Diplomacy helped them avoid fighting on many fronts at once.

For example, if they could keep friendly relations with the Elamites to the south, they would be free to focus on conflicts to the north or east. Similarly, they might have tried to keep trade flowing with Mesopotamia, so they could benefit from the exchange of goods and knowledge. Diplomacy would become even more important when the empire expanded under Cyrus and Darius.

Rise of a United Persian Identity

A key step in the Achaemenid rise was shaping a united Persian identity. Different tribes within Parsa or nearby areas may have had small differences in dialect or custom. The Achaemenid rulers helped bring them together by promoting certain traditions and stories as truly "Persian."

They might have held gatherings or festivals where people came to celebrate common ancestors. They might have encouraged storytelling about legendary heroes who fought for all Persian tribes. This process of building an identity would help them stand strong against outside threats.

Early Achievements and Building Projects

We do not have a lot of records about major building projects before Cyrus the Great. However, it is likely that the Achaemenids started constructing small palaces or administrative centers. They would have also begun the tradition of carving inscriptions to honor their gods or ancestors.

Any such monuments would have shown the strength of their rule. They might have also built roads or rest stops for merchants, as trade was vital. Even though these projects were smaller than what we see in later reigns, they set the tone for how Achaemenid kings would display their power and organize their lands.

The End of Median Supremacy Approaches

By around the mid-6th century BCE, many changes were happening. The Medes were still strong, but they may have become complacent. Their king, Astyages, did not expect a challenge from his Persian relatives or subjects. The Babylonians, under King Nabonidus, were also watching the region closely. Lydia, led by King Croesus, was powerful in the west.

Against this backdrop, the stage was set for a bold leader to rise. That leader was Cyrus II. By building on the political, military, and cultural foundations laid down by previous Achaemenid rulers, he was able to take the final step. He would face Astyages and win, forever changing the balance of power.

What Made the Achaemenids Different

If we compare the Achaemenids to other tribes or families, a few things stand out:

1. **Leadership and Vision**: They had rulers who thought beyond local concerns. They saw opportunities for greater power in a changing world.
2. **Military Skills**: They learned from neighbors, improving their cavalry and archers. They also organized their forces better than many smaller tribes.
3. **Diplomacy**: They did not rush into fights with everyone at once. Instead, they formed alliances and only fought wars they felt they could win.
4. **Cultural Unity**: By promoting Persian identity, they gained the loyalty of people across different tribes.

These strengths set the Achaemenids apart. When the right leader emerged, these pieces fell into place quickly.

Setting the Stage for Cyrus the Great

It is important to note that Cyrus II, later called "the Great," would not have succeeded without the foundations built by men like Teispes, Cyrus I, and Cambyses I. They kept the tribe united, learned from the Medes, and maintained enough independence to preserve their royal line.

Also, the weaknesses of the Medes played a role. Astyages may have ruled harshly, or he might have grown careless in his old age. His nobles might have been ready for a change. Cyrus II was in the perfect position to take advantage of this situation.

Legacy of the Early Achaemenids

Although these early rulers did not conquer large territories, they are still important in the grand story of Persia. Without their efforts to consolidate Persian power in Parsa, there would be no empire for Cyrus the Great to build on. Their story also reminds us that big changes in history often start with small steps taken by people who are preparing for a brighter future.

When we read about Cyrus II in the next chapter, we will see how the seeds planted by his ancestors flourished into a mighty empire. We will also explore the dramatic moments when Cyrus faced the Median king, Astyages, and claimed the throne for himself. That moment was the birth of the Achaemenid Empire as a real force in the ancient world.

CHAPTER 3

CYRUS THE GREAT

Introduction

In the previous chapters, we explored the land before the Persian kings and the early rise of the Achaemenid Dynasty. We learned how small tribes and local rulers, such as those from the House of Achaemenes, laid the groundwork for a much larger empire. Now, we will focus on Cyrus II, best known as **Cyrus the Great**. He is the ruler who truly changed the course of Persian history.

Cyrus the Great is famous for his conquests, but he is also remembered for his fair treatment of the peoples he conquered. He built one of the largest empires in history up to that time, stretching from the edges of Anatolia (in modern Turkey) all the way to Central Asia. His story is full of bravery, clever strategy, and a new kind of leadership that gained respect from many different cultures.

In this chapter, we will look at Cyrus's early life, his rebellion against the Median king Astyages, and his rapid series of victories. We will also examine his ruling style, focusing on how he managed to keep so many different lands under his control. Finally, we will explore his campaigns against Lydia and Babylon, as well as his final battles in the east, which led to his untimely death.

Early Life and Family Ties

As we saw before, Cyrus the Great belonged to the Achaemenid family line. He was probably born around 600 BCE or a bit later, though we do not know the exact year. His father was **Cambyses I**, a

Persian king who ruled a small region called Anshan (or a similar area in southwestern Iran). Some stories say that Cyrus's mother was the daughter or granddaughter of Astyages, the Median king. Whether this is true or not, it shows that the Persians and Medes were closely linked by marriage.

As a child, Cyrus would have grown up hearing stories about heroic ancestors and the glory of the Medes, who were the dominant power at that time. He likely learned horseback riding and archery at a young age, skills that were essential for survival and warfare on the Iranian Plateau. He also would have learned about religion and customs that shaped the Persian identity.

These early lessons helped Cyrus become a strong leader. He understood the way the Medes governed their kingdom because of his family's connections. He also knew how to inspire Persian warriors, who were proud of their heritage. All of this prepared him for the big challenge he would face: standing up to the Median king Astyages and claiming independence for the Persians.

Rebellion Against Astyages

When Cyrus took the Persian throne after his father, Cambyses I, he still recognized the rule of Astyages, at least officially. But tensions between the Persians and Medes were growing. The Medes had been the stronger group for many years, but the Persians were becoming more powerful thanks to better military organization and local support.

There are different stories about how Cyrus's rebellion began. One famous tale, recorded by Greek historians, says that Astyages had a dream or prophecy warning him that his grandson (or a member of his family) would overthrow him. In response, Astyages did many cruel things to try to prevent this from happening. But fate was not on his side, and eventually Cyrus rose up against him.

Whether or not these stories are true, it is clear that Cyrus decided to stop paying tribute to Astyages. The Medes then marched against the Persians to force them back into obedience. However, many Median soldiers were unhappy or did not feel loyal to Astyages. Some even joined Cyrus during the conflict. In the end, Cyrus defeated Astyages around 550 BCE. He captured the Median capital, Ecbatana (present-day Hamadan), and took Astyages prisoner.

This victory was a huge moment. The Medes had once ruled the Persians, but now Cyrus placed the Medes under Persian rule. He did not destroy their land or punish them harshly. Instead, he kept many Median nobles in high positions. By doing so, he showed his style of leadership: firm in victory but willing to respect local customs and elites.

Uniting the Persians and Medes

After defeating Astyages, Cyrus united the Persians and Medes into one kingdom. He allowed the Median aristocrats to keep their wealth and status. This made it easier for them to accept him as their new king. Because the Medes and Persians were culturally similar (they both spoke Indo-Iranian languages and shared certain customs), it was not hard to merge them into a single ruling class.

Cyrus also kept the Median capital, Ecbatana, as an important city. This showed that he did not want to erase the Median heritage but rather include it within his growing realm. In fact, Cyrus often used Median officials in his administration. He learned from their experience governing a large kingdom.

This united force—Medes and Persians together—became the core of Cyrus's new army. It was a strong and loyal group that could face outside threats. With this power base secure, Cyrus turned his eyes toward new lands. He wanted to expand his kingdom and increase his fame.

The Conquest of Lydia

One of the first major targets for Cyrus's expansion was the kingdom of Lydia in Anatolia. Lydia was ruled by **King Croesus**, who was famous for his great wealth. The capital city, Sardis, was a center of trade and culture. Croesus believed he was strong enough to challenge any threat. He also formed alliances with other regional powers, such as Babylon and Egypt, expecting them to help if war broke out.

Croesus was worried that Cyrus's growing power would soon reach Lydia. So, he attacked first, crossing the Halys River (in modern Turkey) to invade territories that Cyrus controlled. However, the war did not go as Croesus had planned. Cyrus responded quickly, leading his army into Lydia. Croesus, thinking he could return to Sardis and gather more troops in the winter, was caught off guard.

Cyrus marched right to the gates of Sardis. The Lydian army fought bravely, but the Persians used clever tactics. According to some sources, they used camels to frighten the Lydian horses. Lydia had a strong cavalry, but the horses got scared of the camels' smell, causing confusion in the Lydian ranks.

Eventually, Sardis fell to Cyrus around 546 BCE. Croesus was captured. Different stories exist about what happened to him. Some say Cyrus treated Croesus kindly and kept him as an advisor. Others suggest that Croesus tried to burn himself, but Cyrus saved him and admired his wisdom. Regardless of the exact details, Lydia was now under Persian control, and Cyrus gained access to the region's wealth and trading networks.

Cyrus's Leadership Style

One of the most striking things about Cyrus was his approach to ruling conquered peoples. Instead of punishing them severely, he often sought to include them in his empire. He allowed local customs and religious practices to continue. He also let some local kings or governors stay in power as long as they pledged loyalty to him.

This style made Cyrus popular in many places. His reputation as a fair and just king spread far and wide. It also helped keep peace in his newly conquered territories. People felt less need to rebel if they were treated with respect. Cyrus also won over local elites by letting them hold important positions and keep some measure of authority.

Because of this approach, Cyrus's empire grew quickly without falling apart. His generals and governors were loyal because they respected him, and the conquered peoples did not rise up in constant revolt. This method of ruling would become a hallmark of the Achaemenid Empire for generations.

The Conquest of Babylon

The most famous of Cyrus's campaigns (after Lydia) was his conquest of Babylon in 539 BCE. Babylon was a major city in Mesopotamia and the heart of the Neo-Babylonian Empire. It was known for its grand architecture, including the famous Hanging Gardens (though these are more legendary than well-documented). The Babylonian king at the time was **Nabonidus**, who had fallen out of favor with many of his own people due to his religious policies.

Cyrus approached Babylon with caution, knowing it was protected by walls and a complex system of canals and rivers. However, he seemed to have gained the support of some Babylonian nobles who were tired of Nabonidus's rule. According to ancient accounts (and there are different versions), the Persians diverted part of the Euphrates River, which flowed through Babylon, lowering the water level enough for Cyrus's troops to enter under the walls.

In October 539 BCE, Babylon fell to the Persian army. The city's population did not put up much of a fight, possibly because they preferred Cyrus to their own king. Cyrus entered the city peacefully, and soon after, Nabonidus was captured.

The Cyrus Cylinder

Not long after taking Babylon, Cyrus issued a declaration that has become famous in modern times. It was written on a clay cylinder, now called the **Cyrus Cylinder**. In it, Cyrus states that he was chosen by the chief Babylonian god, Marduk, to rule Babylon. He also promises to protect the people, respect their temples, and allow them to worship their own gods.

The Cyrus Cylinder is sometimes called the first charter of human rights, though that is more of a modern interpretation. In ancient terms, it served as a statement of legitimacy. Cyrus was saying, "I am the rightful king, and I will govern wisely." This was part of his broader strategy of respect and inclusion.

People in Babylon were allowed to continue their traditions, and local administrators were kept in place. Cyrus even helped some groups who had been forced to move under previous Babylonian kings—like the Jewish people—to return to their homelands if they wished. This gained him support from different communities in the region.

Ruling a Vast Empire

By the time Cyrus conquered Babylon, his empire included:

- The old Median kingdom (including parts of modern Iran)
- The region of Parsa (Persis), his original homeland
- Lydia and parts of Anatolia
- Mesopotamia, including Babylon itself
- Various smaller states that recognized his authority

Managing such a vast area was a challenge. Cyrus used local governors, often called **satraps**, to oversee different provinces. These satraps collected taxes, kept order, and raised troops when needed. But Cyrus also kept watch over them through a system of royal inspectors.

To maintain communication, roads were improved or built. The Royal Road in particular, which stretched from Sardis in the west to the regions near Susa in the east, allowed messengers to carry orders quickly. Travel that once took months could be done in a matter of days with a relay system of fresh horses.

Cyrus also encouraged trade across his empire. By making roads safer and lowering barriers, he boosted economic links between different parts of his domain. People could exchange goods and ideas more freely, and this helped integrate the empire's many cultures.

Religious and Cultural Tolerance

A key part of Cyrus's success was his tolerance of different faiths and customs. Conquered peoples did not have to abandon their gods. They could keep their temples, rituals, and local traditions. This policy reduced the chance of revolts based on religious hatred.

At the same time, Cyrus introduced certain Persian customs to the new lands. This included aspects of the Old Persian language and the royal court etiquette. But he did not force these customs on anyone. Instead, people saw them as part of the royal culture, which they could adopt if they wished to gain favor at court.

Challenges and Further Campaigns

Though Cyrus's empire was growing, it was not without challenges. Some local rulers might break their agreements or refuse to pay tribute. In other cases, new threats emerged on the eastern edges of the empire. Nomadic tribes in Central Asia did not always recognize Persian authority.

Cyrus spent the last years of his life handling these frontier problems. He led campaigns to secure regions in Central Asia, possibly around the Oxus (Amu Darya) River. He might have also pushed further east into areas near modern-day Afghanistan and Pakistan, though details are hazy.

There are also stories that Cyrus battled the **Massagetae**, a nomadic people who lived in the steppe lands northeast of Persia. According to some ancient accounts, their queen, Tomyris, led them in a fierce fight against Cyrus. One version claims that Cyrus was killed in this war, and Tomyris had his head placed in a bag of blood as revenge for the death of her son.

It is hard to know exactly how Cyrus died, but most sources agree that he fell in battle around 530 BCE. His body was brought back and buried in a simple tomb at Pasargadae, which was one of his capital cities. This tomb still exists in Iran today, though we will not focus on modern times.

Cyrus's Legacy

Despite his early death, Cyrus left a lasting mark on the ancient world. He built an empire that was not only large but also relatively stable and fair in its treatment of various peoples. His method of ruling through respect, local autonomy, and efficient administration became the model for later Persian kings.

Many different cultures mention Cyrus in a positive light. The Greek historian Xenophon wrote a work called the **Cyropaedia**, which praises Cyrus as an ideal ruler (though it includes fictional elements). The Old Testament of the Bible describes Cyrus as an instrument of God's will for allowing exiled peoples to return home. Babylonian records, too, speak of him as a liberator.

Because of his policies, Cyrus is remembered as more than just a conqueror. He is often seen as a statesman and a lawgiver who valued justice and mercy. This view may be somewhat romanticized, but it shows how wide his influence was. His empire became a melting pot of cultures, and the seeds he planted would continue to grow under his successors.

Pasargadae and the Beginnings of Imperial Architecture

Cyrus also began building projects that showed Persian power and style. One of the most notable sites from his time is **Pasargadae**, located in the region of Fars. This city had palaces, gardens, and a unique blend of architectural styles—some elements were taken from Median, Elamite, and even Mesopotamian designs.

Pasargadae was important because it was the first capital of the Achaemenid Empire. It served as a symbol of Cyrus's achievements. Though it was not as large or grand as Persepolis (which would be built later by Darius I), it set the pattern for future royal centers. Stone reliefs showed people of different lands meeting in harmony, suggesting that Cyrus wanted to portray his rule as peaceful cooperation among many nations.

Reflection on Cyrus's Character

Historical sources provide different viewpoints about Cyrus's personality. Babylonian texts praise him for his respect of their gods. Greek writers admire his wisdom and bravery. Some Persian traditions see him as a father figure to his people.

Yet we must remember that Cyrus was still a conqueror. He fought wars and defeated rulers who stood in his way. He seized lands and demanded tribute. The difference is that he chose to govern those lands with a lighter touch, giving local populations reason to accept his rule rather than constantly rebel against it.

His approach was groundbreaking for its time and left a model for future empires. Conquerors before him, like the Assyrians, had often relied on fear and harsh treatment. Cyrus showed that another way was possible, a way that might lead to a more stable empire in the long run.

Conclusion of Chapter 3

Cyrus the Great stands as one of the most influential rulers in ancient history. In less than three decades, he united the Persians and Medes, conquered Lydia and Babylon, and extended his reach into Central Asia. His legacy was not just in warfare but in governance. He showed that by respecting local traditions, an empire could expand without constant strife.

Cyrus's sudden death left some unfinished plans, but the empire he built was strong enough to continue. His successors inherited a vast realm and the administrative systems he had set up. In the next chapter, we will look at **Cambyses II**, Cyrus's son, who took the throne after him. We will see how Cambyses expanded the empire further—particularly by taking control of Egypt—but also ran into serious challenges that would shape the future of Persia.

Cyrus's story reminds us that a wise ruler can change the fate of nations. Through courage, diplomacy, and respect for cultural differences, he built the foundation of what would become one of the greatest empires the world has ever known.

CHAPTER 4

CAMBYSES II AND THE EARLY EXPANSION

Introduction

Cyrus the Great had carved out an empire spanning from Asia Minor to the edges of Central Asia. When he died around 530 BCE, his son **Cambyses II** became the next King of Kings. In this chapter, we will focus on Cambyses's rule. We will see how he continued his father's expansionist policies, most notably by conquering Egypt.

However, Cambyses II faced many difficulties as well. While he managed to add more territory to the Achaemenid Empire, he also dealt with unrest at home, military setbacks, and challenges in maintaining the same level of respect Cyrus had earned among conquered peoples. Eventually, Cambyses's reign ended in controversy and mystery, leaving the empire in a state of confusion. This paved the way for the rise of Darius I, whom we will discuss in later chapters.

Cambyses II's Rise to Power

Cambyses II was the eldest son of Cyrus the Great and one of his wives (possibly Cassandane, who was of noble Persian descent). As the crown prince, Cambyses likely served alongside his father in the military campaigns, learning about warfare and governance. When Cyrus died on the battlefield in Central Asia, Cambyses assumed the throne without much trouble—at least at first.

Some sources suggest that Cyrus, before his death, appointed Cambyses as the ruler of Babylon for a short time. If true, this move might have been a way to train Cambyses in managing a major city. It also indicates that Cyrus trusted Cambyses to handle significant responsibilities.

Upon taking power, Cambyses inherited an empire that was large, but still not fully settled. Rebellions could break out if local governors felt they had a chance to break away. Cambyses also had to prove to the nobility and the army that he was worthy of following in his father's footsteps. He knew that conquering new lands, particularly Egypt, could strengthen his reputation and secure his position as king.

Why Egypt?

Egypt was one of the great powers of the ancient world. It was famous for its rich farmland (fed by the Nile River), its gold mines in Nubia, and its grand monuments. By the time of Cambyses, Egypt was ruled by the **26th Dynasty**, with **Pharaoh Psamtik III** (also spelled Psammetichus) on the throne.

Cyrus had planned to invade Egypt but never got the chance due to his campaigns in the east and his final battle. Cambyses decided to carry out this plan. Controlling Egypt would give Persia access to the Nile's wealth and trade routes to Africa. It would also block any alliance between Egypt and other enemies of Persia, such as the Greeks or the Babylonians (though Babylon was already under Persian rule).

From a political point of view, conquering Egypt would show the world that Cambyses was as strong as his father. It would also add another jewel to the Achaemenid crown, making Persia the largest empire of its time.

Preparations for the Egyptian Campaign

Conquering Egypt was not easy. It required a massive invasion force and careful planning. The Persian army had to travel across the Sinai Desert or find sea routes. They needed enough supplies, like food and water, especially for the desert crossing.

Cambyses formed alliances with local tribes who knew the desert routes well. He may have also reached out to certain governors in the eastern parts of the Egyptian realm who were unhappy with the Pharaoh's rule. These alliances helped Cambyses gain safe passage and gather intelligence about Egypt's defenses.

The Persians also built or gathered a fleet, possibly with help from Phoenicians, Greeks from Ionia, and other maritime peoples. This fleet would follow along the coast, bringing supplies and supporting land forces. By combining a strong army with naval support, Cambyses aimed to overwhelm Egypt's defenses.

The Battle of Pelusium

Around 525 BCE, Cambyses and his forces arrived near the eastern edge of Egypt. The Egyptians, led by Pharaoh Psamtik III, set up defenses near Pelusium, which was a key fortress city on the Nile Delta. According to some ancient Greek historians (such as Herodotus), the battle was fierce.

One famous (though possibly legendary) story says that Cambyses, knowing the Egyptians held cats sacred, ordered his soldiers to paint cats on their shields or even carry cats in front of them. Because the Egyptians feared harming these sacred animals, their archers hesitated, giving the Persians an advantage. While this tale may be more myth than fact, it shows how stories grew around Cambyses's conquest of Egypt.

However it happened, the Persians won at Pelusium. The Egyptian forces retreated or were captured, and Psamtik III withdrew to Memphis, near present-day Cairo. Cambyses pressed forward, capturing Heliopolis and then laying siege to Memphis. The city eventually surrendered. Psamtik III was taken prisoner, and Cambyses became the new master of Egypt.

Becoming Pharaoh

Like his father, Cambyses did not simply destroy the lands he conquered. But he also did not show the same level of respect for local traditions as Cyrus did. Even so, he allowed some parts of Egyptian society to continue functioning under Persian oversight. Cambyses crowned himself as Pharaoh, adopting the royal titles. He participated in some Egyptian rituals to legitimize his rule.

However, ancient sources give mixed reports about Cambyses's behavior. Some claim he insulted Egyptian gods, desecrated temples, or behaved cruelly. Others say these accusations might have been exaggerated by later writers who wanted to paint Cambyses in a negative light. We do know that he used Egyptian wealth to pay his army and to secure his power across the empire.

The fact remains that Cambyses successfully ruled Egypt for a short time. Persian administrators began to manage the Nile's resources, collecting taxes and making sure the grain shipments flowed to the empire's core regions. By taking on the title of Pharaoh, Cambyses was trying to follow in Cyrus's footsteps by embracing local customs—at least on a surface level.

Campaigns Beyond Egypt

Eager to expand even further, Cambyses looked to the lands south and west of Egypt. He reportedly sent an army against Nubia (also known as Kush, in the region of modern Sudan). This campaign was very difficult because the Persians had to march through harsh desert lands, and they were not fully prepared with supplies.

Some historical accounts say that part of this Persian army got lost in a sandstorm and vanished. Although these stories might be exaggerated, they suggest that Cambyses's push into Nubia did not go as smoothly as he hoped. Meanwhile, Cambyses also planned an invasion of Carthage in North Africa, but the Phoenicians in his navy refused to attack their own relatives (Carthage was originally founded by Phoenicians). Thus, Cambyses could not rely on his fleet for that campaign, and the plan stalled.

These setbacks showed that while Cambyses had the ambition to enlarge the empire further, he faced real logistical and political problems. The empire was vast, and not all allies were willing to fight against their kin. Harsh environments also made some campaigns nearly impossible to sustain.

Rumors and Rebellions

Back in Persia and other parts of the empire, word began to spread that Cambyses was behaving oddly or harshly in Egypt. Whether these stories were true or exaggerated, they created unease among Persian nobles. Some might have believed that Cambyses was not following the respectful traditions set by Cyrus.

According to Herodotus, Cambyses received news that a rebellion had broken out back in Persia. A man claiming to be **Smerdis** (also called Bardiya), who was supposedly Cambyses's brother, had taken the throne. However, the real Smerdis might have been killed by Cambyses earlier, fearing a challenge to the throne. This meant an imposter could use the name Smerdis to rally support against Cambyses.

When Cambyses heard about the rebellion, he left Egypt quickly to deal with the problem. On his journey back, he either died by accident or was killed under mysterious circumstances around 522 BCE. Different sources offer various explanations: some say he accidentally stabbed himself; others suggest assassination or illness.

Whatever the truth, Cambyses never returned to Persia to confront the rebel in person. His sudden death caused confusion, and the empire faced a serious crisis. Many did not know who ruled Persia now, and some regions might have tried to break away during the chaos.

Cambyses's Character: Myth or Fact?

Ancient historians, especially Greek ones, often wrote about Cambyses in a negative way. They described him as mad, cruel, and disrespectful to gods. They told tales of him slaying sacred animals or killing important priests. Yet we must remember that these sources often aimed to entertain or to push a certain viewpoint. They also lived long after Cambyses's time, so their accounts can be biased or filled with legend.

What we can say for sure is that Cambyses was not as successful as his father in winning the hearts of conquered peoples. But he did manage to conquer and hold Egypt, which was no small feat. He also continued the administrative systems set up by Cyrus, though perhaps with less personal attention to local customs.

Modern scholars still debate Cambyses's true nature. Some think he was ruthless but not insane. Others believe the negative stories came from later Persian kings who wanted to tarnish Cambyses's reputation, making their own reigns look better in comparison. Regardless, Cambyses's time on the throne was marked by both significant conquest and internal instability.

Aftermath of Cambyses's Death

With Cambyses gone, the man calling himself Smerdis remained in control of Persia for a short while. Many people at the time believed he was indeed Cambyses's brother. This new king was accepted by various parts of the empire, since they were unhappy with Cambyses's rule. However, some nobles, including a member of the royal house named **Darius**, doubted this Smerdis's identity.

Before long, Darius and other high-ranking nobles overthrew the imposter. Darius claimed that he was acting to restore the true Achaemenid line. This event is often called the **Magian Revolt** or the **False Smerdis Episode**. Soon, Darius I took the throne, and he had to spend considerable effort putting down rebellions across the empire.

Thus, Cambyses's sudden death and the confusion over Smerdis led to a period of unrest. It was a critical turning point for the Achaemenid Empire. While Cambyses had expanded Persia's borders, the empire was left on shaky ground at the time of his passing.

Administration Under Cambyses

Even during his campaigns, Cambyses had to manage a vast empire. He relied on the satrapy system introduced by Cyrus. Satraps were local governors who collected taxes, oversaw justice, and raised troops in times of war. However, with Cambyses so far away in Egypt, communication and control became harder.

Some satraps may have grown too powerful or felt freer to act on their own. Others stayed loyal but could not fix the empire's problems without clear guidance. Cambyses likely sent letters and messengers, but these took time to travel the great distances. If rumors or rebellions flared up, it could take months for Cambyses to learn about them and respond.

This struggle to keep firm control from afar is one reason why Darius I, when he became king, focused heavily on reorganizing the empire. Darius introduced clearer laws, built more roads, and set up an improved system for watching the satraps. But at this point in our story, Cambyses's methods, though similar to Cyrus's, were not enough to avoid chaos when he left Egypt.

Treatment of Conquered Peoples

Cambyses's reputation for harshness comes mainly from Egyptian sources and Greek accounts. They say he mocked local customs and attacked sacred symbols. However, some modern historians think these stories might have been created or exaggerated by Egyptians who resented foreign rule.

On the other hand, there is evidence that certain Egyptian temples received funds during Cambyses's reign. The Persians needed the support of local priests and officials to govern effectively. Also, Cambyses must have been wise enough to know that if he totally destroyed Egyptian culture, he would face constant revolts.

Thus, while he may not have shown the same deep respect as Cyrus, Cambyses likely allowed many Egyptian institutions to keep operating. He needed local administrators and scribes to manage the day-to-day work of running a kingdom as large and complex as Egypt.

Personal Ambition and Legacy

Cambyses wanted to be seen as a successful conqueror, equal to or greater than his father. Conquering Egypt certainly gave him a big achievement to point to. But his rule lacked the solid foundation of loyalty and admiration that Cyrus had built.

Part of the problem may have been Cambyses's personality. If he was indeed quick-tempered or suspicious (as some sources suggest), that could have driven away trusted advisors. Another issue might have been timing. Cambyses inherited a huge empire that was still in the process of forming. The sudden news of a revolt in Persia at a moment when he was far away in Egypt created a perfect storm of chaos.

By the time Cambyses died, he had made Persia larger but also more unstable. His most lasting legacy is the addition of Egypt to the Achaemenid Empire. This opened the door for new trade routes, cultural exchanges, and strategic positions against future enemies. Even though the empire would see turmoil in the short term, Egypt remained part of the Persian realm for a while, especially during the reign of Darius and later kings.

The Path to Darius I

Cambyses's death and the rise of the false Smerdis set the empire on a dangerous path. Regions from Babylon to Media saw this crisis as a chance to break free. The empire Cyrus had built, and Cambyses had expanded, was in jeopardy.

When Darius I took control, he had to fight multiple rebellions. He claimed legitimacy by pointing out his family ties to the Achaemenid line. In his great inscription at Behistun he explained how he defeated rebels and restored order.

However, this is not yet the story of Darius. For now, we end with Cambyses's last chapter. He may not have been as universally admired as Cyrus, but he made a mark on history by adding Egypt to the empire. His brief reign reminds us that military success alone cannot ensure stability. Wise administration, respect for local customs, and the ability to unify many peoples were all vital for keeping a vast empire together.

Conclusion of Chapter 4

Cambyses II took over a mighty empire from his father, Cyrus the Great. He continued to expand Persian control by conquering Egypt, a major center of wealth and culture. However, his reign was marked by internal strife, rumors of cruelty, and questionable decisions that led to unrest back home. When news of a rebellion reached him, he left Egypt in a hurry, only to die before he could restore order.

This left the empire in disarray, with a false Smerdis claiming the throne. It would fall to Darius I to step in, put down revolts, and guide the empire to its next phase of greatness. Cambyses's story shows that a single leader's personality and choices can affect millions of people. It also proves that conquering new lands is only half the battle—holding them together requires wisdom, respect, and an organized system of government.

CHAPTER 5

DARIUS I AND HIS ADMINISTRATIVE REFORMS

Introduction

In our previous chapters, we explored how Cyrus the Great built a vast empire through respectful governance and military skill, and how his son Cambyses II conquered Egypt but faced unrest that weakened the realm. When Cambyses died suddenly, confusion broke out, and a man claiming to be Smerdis (Cambyses's brother) took the throne. This led many people to question who should truly rule the Persian Empire.

Into this chaos stepped **Darius I**, a member of a noble family connected to the Achaemenid line. Darius quickly put down the false Smerdis and other rebellions. But he did much more than just fight for power—he transformed the Persian Empire. In this chapter, we look at how Darius seized the throne, crushed revolts, and created a complex but well-run government. We see how he built roads, minted coins, and set up local governors called satraps to organize the empire. We also explore his major building projects, such as **Persepolis**, and his early conflicts with the Greek city-states, including the **Ionian Revolt**. By the end, we discover why Darius was often called a "King of Kings," and how his reforms shaped Persia for many years to come.

The Crisis After Cambyses: The Rise of Darius

When Cambyses II hurried back from Egypt to deal with the rebellion in Persia, he died under mysterious circumstances. It left the empire in turmoil. A man who claimed to be **Smerdis**—also spelled Bardiya—began to rule in Cambyses's place. Whether he was a true son of Cyrus or an impostor was unclear, but many regions in the empire accepted him, especially since he promised to lower taxes and reduce burdens on local populations.

Several Persian nobles, however, suspected fraud. Among them was **Darius**, the son of a noble named Hystaspes. Darius insisted that the real Smerdis had been killed long before—likely by Cambyses—and this man on the throne was actually a Magian priest pretending to be Smerdis. Darius allied with a group of other nobles, and together they plotted to overthrow the false king.

The details of how they did this come from later records, notably those written by Darius himself. These accounts might glorify Darius's role, but they do give us a general idea: Darius and a small band of supporters entered the palace, confronted the impostor, and killed him. With the false Smerdis gone, the crown fell to Darius in 522 BCE. However, his hold on power was far from secure because many parts of the empire did not know who he was or why they should follow him.

The Behistun Inscription and Legitimacy

To prove he was the rightful ruler, Darius left a grand statement carved into a mountainside. This carving, known as the **Behistun Inscription**, still exists in western Iran. High up on a cliff face, it shows Darius standing over the captured rebels, with a figure of the god Ahura Mazda floating above him. The text—written in three languages (Old Persian, Elamite, and Babylonian)—explains how Darius defeated the usurpers and many other revolts.

The Behistun Inscription served two main purposes:

1. **Claim of Legitimacy**: Darius declared that he was from the royal line of Achaemenes, and that Ahura Mazda chose him to crush the rebel impostors.
2. **Warning**: Any new rebels could see, carved in stone, what happened to those who challenged the Persian king's authority.

This inscription was an important piece of propaganda, spreading Darius's version of events. By writing it in multiple languages, he made sure people from different areas of the empire could read or hear about his right to rule. As time went on, more and more regions accepted Darius as the new "King of Kings," though not all did so willingly at first.

Rebellions and Consolidation

Despite Darius's dramatic seizure of power, not everyone immediately welcomed him. A series of rebellions broke out across the empire, especially in regions like **Babylon**, **Media**, and **Elam**. Local leaders saw an opportunity to break free from Persian control, given the political chaos.

Darius acted swiftly:

- **Babylon**: A leader claiming to be a relative of the old Babylonian kings arose, hoping to restore local rule. Darius marched there, besieged the city, and recaptured it.
- **Media**: Some Median nobles felt they should be independent again, but Darius defeated them.
- **Elam and Other Regions**: Smaller rebellions also arose, each hoping to cast off Persian domination. One by one, Darius crushed these uprisings.

These victories earned Darius a reputation for strength, but he also understood that force alone would not keep the empire together. People needed stable administration, fair taxes, and a chance to prosper. Once the rebellions were put down, he turned to the big task of organizing and reforming the empire so that future revolts would be less likely.

Administrative Reforms: Satrapies and the Royal Inspectors

One of Darius's most important contributions was refining the **satrapy system**. Satraps were local governors who ruled a province (called a "satrapy") on behalf of the Persian king. This idea existed before Darius, going back to Cyrus the Great, but Darius expanded and improved it.

- **Clear Boundaries**: Darius set up about twenty or more satrapies, each with defined borders.
- **Taxation**: Each satrapy had to pay a fixed amount of tribute to the king, calculated based on the region's resources. This was more organized than the previous, more random ways of collecting taxes.

- **Local Administration**: Satraps often came from local nobility. They knew the region's language and customs, making it easier to govern.
- **Royal Oversight**: To prevent satraps from becoming too powerful or corrupt, Darius appointed separate military commanders and finance officers. These officials did not answer to the satrap but directly to the king.
- **Inspectors (the "Eyes and Ears" of the King)**: Darius sent royal inspectors to travel throughout the empire, often in secret, to check on satraps and other officials. If a governor was abusing power, the inspector could report it back to the king.

This multi-layered system helped keep the vast empire under control. It balanced local autonomy with central oversight, reducing the chance of large-scale rebellions. The people in each satrapy still had some control over their daily affairs, but everyone knew the ultimate authority rested with the "King of Kings," Darius.

Standardizing Coinage, Weights, and Measures

Another major reform by Darius was the introduction of a standard coinage system. Before, various regions might have used local coins, weighed silver, or traded goods. This could be confusing for merchants who traveled across the empire.

- **The Daric**: Darius issued a gold coin called the **daric**, featuring an image of a Persian king or hero holding a bow. A similar silver coin, sometimes called a siglos, was also minted.
- **Reliable Value**: Because the gold content of the daric was consistent, people across the empire trusted it. This made trade easier and faster.
- **Uniform Weights and Measures**: Darius also worked on standardizing weights and measures across satrapies. Common units for length, weight, and volume allowed for fair trade and fewer disputes.

By unifying currency and measurements, Darius boosted commerce between regions like Babylon, Egypt, Anatolia, and beyond. This helped cities grow wealthy, brought tax revenue to the royal treasury, and made distant parts of the empire feel more connected.

Construction Projects: Persepolis, Susa, and More

Darius put a stamp on Persian architecture as well. He built or improved several royal centers, the most famous of which was **Persepolis**. Persepolis served as a ceremonial capital, especially for important festivals and events like the New Year celebration (Nowruz, though in an ancient form).

- **Persepolis**: Located in the Fars region, it included grand palaces, audience halls (apadanas), and impressive relief carvings showing delegates from many lands bringing gifts to the king. The art style blended influences from all across the empire—Median, Mesopotamian, Egyptian, and more—showing Persia's diverse nature.
- **Susa**: Darius also made improvements to **Susa**, an older Elamite city. He built a new palace complex there, and it became a major administrative hub. Because Susa was closer to Mesopotamia, it was handy for governing the empire's western and central territories.
- **Canals and Roads**: Darius is credited with completing a canal linking the Nile River to the Red Sea, improving trade and military movement by water. He also built or upgraded roads, including famous routes like the **Royal Road** from Sardis to Susa, which allowed messengers to travel very quickly for the time.

Through these projects, Darius showcased Persian power and provided the infrastructure for effective rule. Buildings like Persepolis symbolized the empire's wealth and unity under the king. Roads and canals turned that unity into reality by tying distant regions together.

Communication and the Royal Road

One of Darius's greatest achievements was improving long-distance communication. Over such a large empire, sharing news and orders could otherwise take months. Darius's roads and messenger system sped this process up:

1. **Relay Stations**: Along the Royal Road, Darius built stations where fresh horses and riders waited. A messenger could swap a tired horse for a fresh one, continuing the journey without delay.
2. **Security**: Persian soldiers and officials patrolled the roads to keep bandits away, making travel safer for merchants, travelers, and government couriers.
3. **Speed**: Ancient historians wrote that messages could travel from one end of the empire to the other in just days, an impressive feat for the time.

This swift communication allowed Darius to respond to crises quickly, whether it was a local rebellion or a threat from outside. It also encouraged trade because merchants knew they could move along relatively safe and well-maintained routes. All these factors strengthened both the economy and the king's control.

The Ionian Revolt

Darius's empire stretched into Anatolia (modern Turkey), where many Greek city-states existed under Persian rule. The Persians allowed these cities to govern themselves in some ways, but they still had to pay taxes and obey Persian-appointed rulers called tyrants. Over time, resentment grew among the Greek cities, especially in Ionia (the coastal region facing the Aegean Sea).

In 499 BCE, a rebellion called the **Ionian Revolt** broke out. Several Greek cities, including Miletus, rose against Persian control. They received some limited help from Athens and other Greek city-states, though not as much as they might have hoped. The Ionian Revolt lasted until about 494 BCE, with the Persians eventually crushing it.

Darius was angered by the support Athens had given to the rebels. Although the rebellion in Ionia was put down, it planted the seed for future conflict between Persia and the Greek mainland. Darius decided that punishing Athens would show all his subjects that no one could aid rebels without consequence. This decision set the stage for the famous Persian Wars with Greece.

The First Conflict with Athens

After subduing the Ionian cities, Darius turned his sights on Athens. He sent a Persian force to attack the Greek mainland. In 490 BCE, the Persians landed at **Marathon**, not far from Athens. They expected to defeat the smaller Athenian force easily. However, the Athenians surprised them by attacking quickly and fiercely, using tight battle formations called phalanxes.

In the **Battle of Marathon**, the Persian army suffered a sharp defeat. The Athenians, though outnumbered, fought with determination on their own land. Persian forces withdrew, marking a setback for Darius's expansion westward. While this loss did not threaten Darius's hold on the empire as a whole, it was a blow to his prestige. It also showed the Greeks that Persia, though formidable, could be challenged.

Despite the defeat at Marathon, Darius continued to rule a vast and wealthy empire. But the conflict with Greece was not over. Darius began to prepare another expedition, this time on a larger scale. He also had to contend with unrest in other parts of the empire. Shortly afterward, Darius's health began to fail.

Darius's Later Reign and Final Years

Even with the setback in Greece, Darius remained a busy ruler in his final years. He continued to refine the administration of the empire, gathering taxes and resources to fund future campaigns. He built new constructions at Persepolis and ensured that other major cities, like Babylon and Ecbatana, remained loyal.

However, Darius grew older, and his plan for a renewed invasion of Greece had to wait. In 486 BCE, he died, leaving the throne to his son, **Xerxes I**. By the time of his death, Darius had shaped the empire in ways that would last long after him:

- He had expanded it from parts of modern Pakistan in the east to the edges of Egypt and Anatolia in the west.
- He had built a sophisticated administration that balanced local governance with central control.
- He had promoted the use of a unified currency, stable roads, and a courier system that helped keep the empire connected.
- He had begun a conflict with the Greek city-states that would play a major role in the next generation of Persian rulers.

The Legacy of Darius: The "King of Kings"

Darius I is often remembered as the organizer of the Achaemenid Empire. While Cyrus the Great founded the empire and Cambyses added Egypt, Darius took these conquests and gave them a lasting structure. Through his reforms, he turned a loose collection of conquered lands into a single, interconnected realm.

People in Persia and beyond admired Darius's administrative skills. The roads, coinage, and bureaucracy he set up made life easier for merchants, travelers, and officials. Even in lands far from the imperial center, people benefited from more efficient trade and fewer local disputes over taxes and measures. The idea of a "universal" empire—one that recognized many cultures but was governed by a single mighty king—found strong footing under his rule.

Of course, Darius was also a conqueror who used force to suppress rebellions. He did not hesitate to crush opponents who challenged him, and he demanded high taxes to fund his court and armies. But many of those taxes went to building projects and improvements that could, in turn, benefit the regions under his control. His approach was a mix of strength and statecraft that many later rulers tried to copy.

CHAPTER 6

XERXES I AND THE WARS WITH GREECE

Introduction

With Darius I's death in 486 BCE, his son **Xerxes I** ascended the throne of the Persian Empire. Xerxes inherited a vast domain stretching from the Indus Valley to the edges of the Aegean Sea. He also inherited a conflict with the Greek city-states, which his father had begun—particularly due to their involvement in the Ionian Revolt and the Persian defeat at the Battle of Marathon.

In this chapter, we explore Xerxes's early reign, including rebellions in Egypt and Babylon that tested his authority. We then turn to his grand campaign against Greece, which brought some of the most famous battles in ancient history: **Thermopylae**, **Salamis**, and later **Plataea**. We will see how Xerxes prepared a massive invasion force, the challenges he faced in foreign lands, and why his campaign ultimately failed to bring Greece under Persian control. Finally, we will touch on Xerxes's later years—his building projects, court intrigues, and the circumstances of his death. Through this story, we discover a ruler with enormous resources but also enormous challenges, whose ambitions shaped the empire's future direction.

Xerxes's Succession: Early Rebellions

When Xerxes came to power, he was around 30 years old. Despite his father's careful planning, Xerxes's rule was not without opposition. Two major rebellions broke out almost immediately:

1. **Egyptian Revolt**: Egypt, added to the empire by Cambyses II, had always been proud of its long history and culture. Some Egyptians saw the change of Persian kings as a chance to regain independence. Xerxes responded by crushing this revolt decisively, removing any Egyptian pharaoh-like titles he might have used. He placed Egypt under stricter control to prevent future uprisings.

2. **Babylonian Revolt**: Babylon, once a grand kingdom under Nebuchadnezzar, also tried to break away. Rebels crowned their own "king" in opposition to Xerxes. Like his father, Xerxes marched against Babylon. After restoring order, he reportedly treated Babylon more harshly than Darius had, removing the golden statue of the Babylonian chief god, Marduk, and taking it away. Some sources say he even damaged parts of Babylon's famous temples.

These actions showed that Xerxes ruled in a more forceful, sometimes harsher way than his father. He might have felt the need to do this because he was still proving himself to the empire's nobility and military leaders. By stamping out rebellions quickly, he demonstrated that he would not tolerate disobedience. However, these measures also caused resentment among some subjects, who saw Xerxes as less tolerant of local traditions than Darius or Cyrus had been.

Preparing for the Invasion of Greece

Xerxes's decision to invade Greece came as an extension of his father's plans. Darius had intended to punish Athens for helping the Ionian cities revolt and for the Persian loss at Marathon. Xerxes, after dealing with the revolts in Egypt and Babylon, turned his full attention to this project.

- **Building a Massive Army**: Ancient sources claim Xerxes gathered forces from all corners of the empire—Persians, Medes, Elamites, Egyptians, Babylonians, Phoenicians, and more. While the ancient numbers are likely exaggerated (some writers mention millions of soldiers), there is no doubt Xerxes commanded a huge army by the standards of the time.
- **Naval Power**: The Persian fleet was crucial because Greece is surrounded by sea. Xerxes gathered ships from Phoenicia, Ionia, Egypt, and other regions. The Persian navy, like the army, was diverse and large.
- **Bridging the Hellespont**: One of the most famous engineering feats was Xerxes's building of floating bridges across the **Hellespont** (the narrow strait now called the Dardanelles) to move his troops from Asia to Europe. When the first set of bridges was destroyed by a storm, Xerxes famously punished the waters by whipping them—an act later Greek sources mocked. He then built new bridges that worked, allowing his forces to cross into Thrace and continue south toward Greece.
- **Supply and Logistics**: Xerxes established depots along the route so that his army could be fed. Herds of animals were sent ahead, and storage points were stocked with grain. This level of organization suggests Xerxes learned from Darius's strong administrative systems.

By 480 BCE, Xerxes's forces were ready. Many Greek city-states were alarmed. Some, like Thessaly, submitted to Xerxes, while others, notably Athens and Sparta, formed alliances to defend their homeland. The stage was set for a historic clash.

The Greek Campaign: Thermopylae

As Xerxes advanced, a small Greek force under Spartan King **Leonidas** blocked his path at **Thermopylae**, a narrow pass between mountains and sea. For days, the vastly outnumbered Greeks held off the Persian army. Their tight phalanx formations forced the Persians to attack in a narrow space, reducing the Persian numerical advantage.

Eventually, a local Greek showed Xerxes a secret path around the pass. When the Persians outflanked them, Leonidas realized the battle was lost. He sent most of the Greek troops away to fight another day, staying behind with a small band—mainly Spartans—to hold off the Persians as long as possible. Leonidas and his men died heroically, but their resistance delayed Xerxes and became a symbol of Greek courage.

Thermopylae was a tactical Persian victory; the way south to Athens was now open. But it was also a moral boost for the Greeks, showing that a small, disciplined force could stand against the huge Persian army. Xerxes pushed on, determined to crush any remaining Greek resistance.

The Naval Battle of Salamis

While Xerxes marched south, the Persian navy followed along the coast. Athens had been evacuated, with most citizens fleeing to the island of Salamis and nearby places. The Persian army reached Athens and burned parts of the city, including sacred temples on the Acropolis, as punishment for their defiance. But the real test came at sea.

The Greek navy, under the command of Athenian general **Themistocles**, lured the larger Persian fleet into the narrow straits near Salamis. In tight waters, the Persian ships could not maneuver effectively. The lighter, faster Greek triremes rammed and sank many Persian vessels. Xerxes, watching from a throne set on a hill, saw his navy suffer a devastating defeat.

The **Battle of Salamis** in 480 BCE was a turning point. Without naval control, Xerxes's ability to supply his large army in Greece became difficult. Worried about potential revolts back in Persia and the threat of winter, Xerxes withdrew most of his forces, leaving a general named Mardonius to continue the war. But Xerxes himself returned east, never personally leading another campaign into Greece.

The Battle of Plataea and the Persian Retreat

Mardonius and the remaining Persian forces tried to finish the conquest of Greece in 479 BCE. However, the Greek city-states united once more and defeated the Persians at the **Battle of Plataea**. Around the same time, the Greek fleet also won a victory at Mycale in Ionia, driving out or destroying Persian ships and encouraging more Ionian cities to revolt again.

With these defeats, Persia effectively lost control over the Greek mainland. Though it kept some influence in parts of the Aegean region and Asia Minor, the dream of adding Greece as a fully conquered province slipped away. For Xerxes, the wars with Greece had become a costly venture that strained the empire's resources and morale.

Effects of the War on the Empire

Xerxes's campaign against Greece had several major results:

1. **Financial Strain**: Maintaining a giant army and navy was expensive, and the war did not bring back riches to offset the costs.

2. **Loss of Prestige**: Xerxes had boasted of punishing Athens and bringing all Greece under his rule. The setbacks at Salamis and Plataea damaged his reputation as an invincible monarch.
3. **Greek Confidence**: The Greeks gained confidence. Their city-states united (though still quarrelsome) around the idea of freedom from Persian rule. In the coming decades, Athens in particular grew strong, setting the stage for the classical period of Greek power and culture.
4. **End of Large Western Campaigns**: After Xerxes, future Persian kings would not launch invasions on the same massive scale into mainland Greece. While conflicts continued around the Aegean Sea, there was no second attempt at a grand conquest of the Greek peninsula.

Still, the Persian Empire remained huge and strong in many other regions. Xerxes returned to a life of ruling over vast territories, collecting tribute, and building monumental works in the heartland.

Xerxes's Building Projects and Court Life

Despite the failures in Greece, Xerxes invested in major building projects, especially at Persepolis. He expanded on what his father Darius had started, adding new palaces, halls, and gateways:

- **The Gate of All Nations**: A grand entrance to the Persepolis complex, featuring carved winged bulls and inscriptions in three languages. It symbolized the empire's diversity.
- **Hall of a Hundred Columns**: One of the largest roofed halls of the ancient world, used for big ceremonies and gatherings of nobles.
- **Decorative Reliefs**: Xerxes continued the tradition of showing people from many nations bringing gifts to the Persian king, reinforcing the idea of a united empire under one supreme ruler.

Xerxes also maintained the splendid royal court, where nobles from across the empire would visit, bringing tributes and seeking favors. The Persian court was known for its protocol, feasts, and ceremonies. However, it was also a place of intrigue. Rivalries among nobles and royal family members could lead to plots and assassinations.

Xerxes's Later Reign: Intrigues and Death

As Xerxes grew older, his focus turned less to conquest and more to internal matters. Ancient Greek sources claim he became distracted by palace life, leaving much of the day-to-day ruling to advisers. Whether this is true or an exaggeration, we know Xerxes had to manage ongoing issues, such as occasional unrest in provinces and the challenge of keeping the empire's satraps loyal.

The end of Xerxes's life was violent. Around 465 BCE, he was murdered in a court plot led by one of his officials, possibly the commander of his royal bodyguard. The reasons behind this assassination are not fully clear—maybe political rivalry, maybe personal vengeance. After Xerxes's death, his son **Artaxerxes I** took the throne, continuing the Achaemenid line but also inheriting the challenges left by years of warfare and internal intrigue.

Conclusion of Chapter 6

Xerxes I inherited a powerful empire from Darius I but also a difficult task: avenging the Persian defeat at Marathon and expanding the empire into Greece. He managed to field one of the largest armies of the ancient world, crossing the Hellespont on remarkable floating bridges and winning a dramatic victory at Thermopylae. Yet his successes ended with a disastrous naval loss at Salamis and eventual defeat on land at Plataea.

Those defeats not only halted Persian expansion into Europe but also tarnished Xerxes's reputation. They showed that the empire, vast as it was, could be resisted by smaller but determined and well-organized groups. Xerxes returned home to focus on building projects, including grand additions to Persepolis, and on keeping his empire united. However, palace intrigues ultimately cut his life short. He left behind a legacy as a mighty king who attempted an ambitious conquest but fell short in achieving his greatest goal.

CHAPTER 7

LATER ACHAEMENID RULERS AND THE FALL OF THE EMPIRE

Introduction

In our last chapter, we watched Xerxes I lead a huge army into Greece, win at Thermopylae, but then lose at the battles of Salamis and Plataea. He returned home to rule the Persian Empire until his death in 465 BCE. After Xerxes, the Achaemenid Empire went through many ups and downs. Different kings took the throne, each with his own challenges—rebellions in the provinces, conflicts with Greek city-states, and power struggles at the royal court.

In this chapter, we will explore how these later Achaemenid kings tried to keep the empire strong, even as new problems arose. We will see the rise of kings like Artaxerxes I, Darius II, Artaxerxes II, Artaxerxes III, and a few others. We will learn how they handled revolts at home, fought wars abroad, and made treaties with their Greek rivals. As time went on, the empire faced growing pressure from outside forces and from within. We will end by setting the stage for the final Achaemenid king, Darius III, who faced the greatest threat of all: Alexander the Great of Macedon.

Artaxerxes I: Stabilizing After Xerxes (465–424 BCE)

When Xerxes I was killed in 465 BCE, his son **Artaxerxes I** took the throne. Artaxerxes I inherited a large but somewhat shaken empire. Xerxes had left behind a legacy of costly wars with Greece and harsh rule in places like Babylon. Many nobles saw an opportunity to gain more power, and some provinces were restless.

Dealing with Court Intrigue

Artaxerxes I faced internal plots soon after becoming king. Some members of the royal family or high-ranking officials had their own ambitions. The Persians had a long tradition of noble families holding large estates and commanding troops, so any sign of weakness from the king invited rebellion. Artaxerxes took steps to secure his throne by rewarding loyal nobles and punishing those who conspired against him.

Challenges in the West: Ongoing Greek Conflicts

Though Xerxes had failed to conquer the Greek mainland, Persia still controlled parts of Asia Minor where many Greek cities were located. These cities often looked to Athens or Sparta for help, hoping to free themselves from paying tribute to Persia. Athens, a rising naval power, had built the **Delian League**, a group of city-states that pledged to keep fighting the Persians.

During Artaxerxes I's reign, Athens sent forces to support rebellions in Egypt (which was always eager to break away) and in Cyprus. The Persians managed to put down these revolts, but the cost was high. In the 450s BCE, the famous Athenian general Cimon led an attack on Cyprus, but Athenian support began to wane. Finally, around 449 BCE, the **Peace of Callias** was supposedly agreed upon (though modern scholars debate its exact details). This peace reduced open warfare between Athens and Persia for a while.

Building Projects and Administration

Artaxerxes I also continued work on royal cities, including Susa and Persepolis. He wanted to show that Persia remained strong despite earlier defeats in Greece. Like his predecessors, he depended on the satrapy system to run the empire. Satraps collected taxes, kept local order, and raised troops when needed. Artaxerxes tried to ensure they were loyal by placing close friends or relatives in important positions.

By the time Artaxerxes I died in 424 BCE, he had kept the empire mostly intact. Although there were tensions with Athens and revolts in Egypt, Persia still stretched from the Indus River to the Aegean Sea and from Central Asia down to the Nile. But the seeds of future problems were there—ambitious satraps, repeated revolts in places like Egypt, and a lingering rivalry with the Greeks.

Darius II: A Time of Court Struggles (424–404 BCE)

After Artaxerxes I passed away, the empire fell into a short period of confusion. Several of Artaxerxes' sons or relatives claimed the throne, leading to assassinations and palace power plays. Eventually, **Darius II** (sometimes called Darius II Ochus) emerged as the new king around 423 or 424 BCE.

Revolts and Unrest

Darius II's reign was marked by constant problems. Egypt revolted again, and the local leaders declared independence. Persian attempts to recapture Egypt mostly failed during Darius II's time. This loss of Egypt was a big blow, both in terms of prestige and the wealth that Egypt provided from its fertile lands.

In Asia Minor, some satraps became very powerful, acting almost like independent rulers. They made local alliances, taxed their subjects heavily, and sometimes resisted the king's orders. Darius II had trouble reining in these satraps because he also needed them to keep the Greeks in check and to send troops for wars elsewhere. It was a balancing act that often left the central government weaker.

Involvement in the Peloponnesian War

Meanwhile, the Greek world was consumed by the **Peloponnesian War** (431–404 BCE), mainly between Athens and Sparta. The Persians saw an opportunity in this conflict. If Athens and Sparta were fighting each other, they had less time to bother Persia.

Darius II tried to play one Greek side against the other. He offered funds to whichever side would serve Persia's interests. At first, he might support Sparta if they promised to stay out of Asia Minor, but if Sparta got too strong, Persia might switch to Athens. This policy aimed to keep the Greeks divided and weaker.

In the end, Darius II supported Sparta heavily by giving gold to help Sparta build a navy. That navy then defeated Athens at sea. In 404 BCE, Athens surrendered. From the Persian point of view, this was a success—one major Greek power was humbled. But the policy of fueling Greek wars also allowed satraps in Asia Minor to grow more independent, as they made their own deals with Greek generals.

Court Intrigue and Death

Darius II also faced trouble at his own court. Palace officials and even members of the royal family fought for control and favor. Darius II grew ill and died in 404 BCE, leaving the throne to his son, **Artaxerxes II**. The empire was still large, but its hold on places like Egypt had slipped. Unrest among the satraps posed a serious threat. There were also fresh problems brewing in the Greek world, especially with the rise of Sparta as a major power.

Artaxerxes II: The Long Reign (404–359 BCE)

Artaxerxes II, also called Artaxerxes II Mnemon, ruled for about 45 years, one of the longest reigns in Achaemenid history. His time as king was filled with wars against his own brother, conflicts with Greek city-states, and constant satrap revolts. Yet he managed to hold the empire together through diplomacy and a mix of strong and lenient policies.

The Revolt of Cyrus the Younger

Shortly after Artaxerxes II became king, his younger brother **Cyrus the Younger** challenged his right to rule. Cyrus gathered an army that included many Greek mercenaries, hoping to overthrow Artaxerxes. The two armies met at **Cunaxa** in 401 BCE, near Babylon.

In the battle, Cyrus fought bravely but was killed. His Greek mercenaries, known as the "Ten Thousand," found themselves stranded deep in Persian territory. They managed to fight their way back to the Black Sea, an event described by the Greek writer Xenophon in **Anabasis**. For Artaxerxes II, this was a relief—his brother's revolt ended quickly. Still, the incident showed how Greek warriors could be hired by Persian rebels, posing a real danger.

Greek Interference and the King's Peace

Even though Cyrus the Younger's revolt failed, the Greek city-states in Asia Minor continued to cause trouble. Sparta, victorious after the Peloponnesian War, tried to extend its power into Persian lands. Artaxerxes II responded by funding Sparta's enemies in Greece, eventually leading to conflicts between Sparta and other Greek powers like Thebes and Athens.

All this fighting forced the Greeks to come to terms with Persia in 386 BCE, resulting in the **King's Peace** (also called the Peace of Antalcidas). In this treaty, Artaxerxes II demanded that all Greek cities in Asia Minor be returned to Persian control, and that other Greek cities remain independent, stopping them from forming strong alliances. This deal showed that Persia could still influence Greek affairs.

However, peace in the Greek world did not mean peace for Persia as a whole. The empire's size and diverse populations meant that revolts and intrigues never fully stopped. Artaxerxes II spent much of his reign putting down rebellions by satraps who wanted more freedom or who aligned themselves with discontented members of the royal family.

Struggles in Egypt and Other Provinces

Egypt stayed out of Persian hands during most of Artaxerxes II's time on the throne. Attempts to reconquer it either failed or ended in stalemates. The Nile region was too well-defended, and Persian generals could not break the local rulers' hold.

In other areas, such as Phrygia and Lydia (in Asia Minor), powerful satraps sometimes acted like mini-kings. They collected taxes, kept large armies, and even made deals with Greek cities without asking the Great King. Artaxerxes II tried to manage this by playing satraps off one another or replacing them with more loyal subjects. Yet the empire's far corners continued to test the king's authority.

Artaxerxes II's Later Years

Despite all these challenges, Artaxerxes II's long reign brought a kind of stability. He was known for using diplomacy and wealth to solve problems rather than always resorting to war. He was also a builder, adding to palace complexes at Persepolis and Susa. By the time he died in 359 BCE, Persia still stood as a major power in the ancient world, but the empire was growing weaker internally.

Artaxerxes III: A Brief Resurgence (359–338 BCE)

When **Artaxerxes III** (originally named Ochus) took power in 359 BCE, he quickly moved to eliminate rivals within the royal family. He was more ruthless than some of his predecessors, believing strong actions were needed to keep the empire together.

Crushing Satrap Revolts

Artaxerxes III forced many satraps to swear renewed loyalty. He also dismissed or executed those who seemed too independent. This gave him tighter control, at least for a while. He waged campaigns to subdue regions that had become nearly self-governing. Though harsh, his methods restored a sense of central authority.

Reconquest of Egypt

One of Artaxerxes III's biggest successes was recapturing Egypt in 343 BCE. After decades of unsuccessful attempts by earlier kings, his strong army and careful planning finally brought the Nile region back under Persian rule. This boosted the empire's prestige and brought back Egypt's resources, including its wealth and grain.

However, the re-conquest did not earn the love of the Egyptians. They deeply resented foreign rule and the heavy taxes that came with it. Artaxerxes III tried to secure Egypt by placing Persian officials in key positions, but Egypt remained a tense province. Local revolts kept popping up, and the Persian army had to stay on guard.

End of Artaxerxes III

Artaxerxes III's strict rule made him many enemies. After only about 20 years on the throne, he was reportedly poisoned by a high court official named Bagoas in 338 BCE. His death once again threw the royal court into turmoil. Different factions backed different princes, and assassinations became common. Meanwhile, in the Greek world, a new power was rising: **Macedonia**, led by King Philip II, and soon by his son **Alexander the Great**.

The Last Kings: Artaxerxes IV and Arses

After Artaxerxes III's murder, Bagoas the court official placed a new king on the throne, **Artaxerxes IV** (also called Arses). This young ruler had little real power. Bagoas ran the court from behind the scenes. In a short time, Bagoas decided to remove Artaxerxes IV as well, possibly by poisoning him.

Bagoas then installed another young member of the royal family as king, who took the name **Darius III**. Bagoas hoped to control him, too. But the new king proved stronger than expected. Once he felt secure, Darius III forced Bagoas to drink poison. That ended the old official's meddling. But Darius III soon faced a much bigger threat that would test the very survival of the Achaemenid Empire.

Darius III and the Looming Storm

Darius III came to the throne around 336 BCE, at a time when Philip II of Macedon had already united most of Greece under Macedonian influence. After Philip II was assassinated, his young son **Alexander** became king. Though only in his early twenties, Alexander was ambitious and had a skilled army, trained by Philip to fight in a new and powerful style.

Darius III tried to secure his reign. He dealt with minor rebellions and reorganized the court. But soon, Alexander declared war on Persia, claiming to free the Greek cities in Asia Minor from Persian control. In 334 BCE, Alexander crossed the Hellespont with a Macedonian and Greek army. This began the most famous war in Achaemenid history—and signaled the final countdown for Persia's greatest empire.

Setting the Stage for the Final Conflict

Darius III gathered his forces, but the empire was not as strong as it had once been under Cyrus or Darius I. Many satraps remembered their own ambitions. Some provinces resented heavy taxes. The Greek mercenaries that Persia often hired were now on Alexander's side or were unwilling to fight a well-led Macedonian force.

Moreover, Darius III did not have much time to train new troops or prepare a coherent strategy. Alexander moved quickly, winning battles at the **Granicus River** (334 BCE) and then taking control of much of Asia Minor. News of these victories spread fast, encouraging more of the local cities to welcome Alexander. Darius III prepared to meet Alexander in a grand showdown, but the odds were not in his favor.

Conclusion of Chapter 7

The years after Xerxes I were a time of both continuity and slow decline for the Achaemenid Empire. Kings like Artaxerxes I, Darius II, and Artaxerxes II kept the empire together with careful diplomacy and, sometimes, force. Artaxerxes III briefly revived Persian power, even retaking Egypt, but court plots weakened the royal house. By the time Darius III took the throne, the empire faced a new and frightening rival: Alexander of Macedon, leading a disciplined army and backed by Greek city-states that had grown stronger.

CHAPTER 8

ALEXANDER THE GREAT AND THE END OF ACHAEMENID RULE

Introduction

In the previous chapter, we saw how the Achaemenid Empire struggled under various rulers after Xerxes I. Rebellions flared, satraps grew powerful, and the royal court was filled with plots. Finally, **Darius III** took the throne, but by then, a rising power in the west—Macedonia—was already poised to strike. Under the young and ambitious **Alexander the Great**, the Macedonians aimed to topple Persia and seize its vast lands.

In this chapter, we will follow Alexander's swift and daring conquest of the Achaemenid Empire. We will examine the key battles—Granicus, Issus, and Gaugamela—where Persian forces fought bravely but could not overcome Alexander's tactics and leadership. We will see how Darius III tried to defend his realm, only to face betrayal and collapse. Finally, we will observe Alexander's decision to burn Persepolis, his pursuit of Darius, and the moment when the Achaemenid Empire effectively ended. By exploring this crucial time, we learn how a once-mighty empire can fall under the pressure of an unstoppable foe and how the world changed as Greek and Persian cultures mixed in the wake of Alexander's victory.

The Rise of Alexander

Before taking on Persia, Alexander had to secure his throne in Macedonia. His father, **Philip II**, had turned Macedonia into a strong kingdom with a reformed army. Philip was assassinated in 336 BCE, and Alexander became king. Some Greek city-states saw this as a chance to break free from Macedonian rule, but Alexander crushed their rebellions quickly, showing he was just as capable as his father—if not more so.

Alexander also inherited Philip's plan to invade the Persian Empire. Officially, the Greeks claimed they wanted revenge for the Persian invasions of Greece in the past, but many sought wealth and glory as well. Alexander used both reasons to rally support.

By 334 BCE, Alexander was ready. He led an army of about 35,000 men across the Hellespont into Asia Minor, symbolically throwing a spear into the ground and claiming the land as his. It was a bold declaration that Macedonia was coming for the entire Persian realm.

The Battle of the Granicus River (334 BCE)

The first major clash happened at the **Granicus River** in northwestern Asia Minor. Persian satraps in the region gathered their forces to stop Alexander at the riverbank. The Persians placed themselves on higher ground, expecting the Macedonians to struggle while crossing the river.

Alexander, known for his personal bravery, led a cavalry charge straight through the river, surprising the Persian cavalry. The Macedonian phalanx followed, pushing aside Persian infantry. Although the Persians fought fiercely, they were outmaneuvered and forced to retreat.

Aftermath of Granicus

This victory gave Alexander control of much of Asia Minor in a short time. Greek cities under Persian control saw Alexander as a liberator. Some Persian garrisons surrendered, hoping for lenient treatment. Alexander, for his part, tried to win local support by keeping the cities' governments in place, only insisting they support his campaign and abandon Persian rule.

Darius III, alarmed by the speed of Alexander's advance, began gathering a larger army to defend the empire. He realized that small, separate satrap forces were no match for Alexander's united Macedonian army. Darius decided to lead the Persian forces himself in the next major battle.

The Battle of Issus (333 BCE)

Darius III chose to meet Alexander near **Issus**, a narrow coastal plain in the southeastern part of Asia Minor. Persian sources say Darius brought a massive army, far outnumbering Alexander's. However, the terrain at Issus worked against the Persians. Their large force had trouble deploying effectively in the tight space between the mountains and the sea.

When the battle started, Darius positioned himself in the center, hoping to oversee his army and inspire his troops. Alexander directed his cavalry to strike at weak points in the Persian lines. The Macedonian phalanx locked shields and advanced steadily, while Alexander led a daring cavalry attack aimed at the heart of the Persian formation.

Seeing the Macedonian advance, Darius III panicked—legend says he left the battlefield in haste when the fighting grew intense near him. This caused confusion among the Persian troops, who began to retreat. Many thousands of Persian soldiers were lost, and some of Darius's family members—his mother, wife, and children—were captured by Alexander.

Impact of Issus

The defeat at Issus was a huge blow to Persian morale. Darius's flight made him appear weak, and Alexander's reputation soared. The Persian royal family, now in Alexander's care, was treated respectfully, showing that Alexander wanted to be seen as a noble conqueror rather than a cruel invader.

Darius offered to pay ransom for his family and cede large parts of the empire west of the Euphrates to Alexander in exchange for peace. But Alexander refused, insisting he would settle matters by conquering the entire Persian Empire. He then marched south toward Phoenicia and Egypt, knowing that controlling the coastline would prevent Persian fleets from attacking Greece by sea.

The Conquest of the Eastern Mediterranean and Egypt

After Issus, many coastal cities in Phoenicia surrendered, though the island city of Tyre resisted fiercely. Alexander besieged Tyre for seven months (332 BCE), building a causeway out to the island and eventually capturing it. This victory opened the way to Egypt, which had always been a target for both the Persians and the Greeks.

Egypt Under Alexander

When Alexander arrived in Egypt, the local population greeted him as a liberator from Persian rule. Many Egyptians disliked Persian governors, who imposed heavy taxes and, in their view, disrespected Egyptian religion. Alexander took a different approach. He made offerings to Egyptian gods and visited the oracle of Amun at Siwa Oasis, where priests hailed him as the son of a god.

In early 331 BCE, Alexander founded the city of **Alexandria** near the Nile delta, envisioning it as a center of Greek culture and trade. He then left Egypt, secure in the belief that the Egyptians were on his side. Meanwhile, Darius III gathered yet another large army in Mesopotamia, hoping for one more great showdown that could save the empire.

The Battle of Gaugamela (331 BCE)

The decisive battle took place near **Gaugamela**, in what is now northern Iraq, in October 331 BCE. Darius chose a flat, open plain where the Persian cavalry could maneuver. He even ordered the ground smoothed out to help his chariots, which were fitted with scythes on the wheels to cut into enemy lines.

Alexander's army was smaller but highly disciplined. He arranged his phalanx in the center and placed cavalry on the wings. Darius's army included cavalry, infantry from many regions of the empire, elephants, and the feared scythed chariots.

When the battle began, Darius tried to outflank Alexander using chariots and large numbers of cavalry. However, Alexander's light troops and archers disrupted the chariots, and his skilled horsemen kept the Persian cavalry busy. Then Alexander led a bold charge toward the gap in the Persian lines near Darius's position. Fearing capture or death, Darius lost heart and fled again, as at Issus.

Aftermath of Gaugamela

With Darius gone, the Persian troops lost their will to fight. The Macedonians claimed a decisive victory. Many historians see Gaugamela as the end of the Achaemenid Empire's real power. The road to Babylon, Susa, and eventually Persepolis lay open to Alexander. Local satraps, seeing the king defeated, hurried to make peace with the invader.

Darius III retreated east, hoping to gather new forces, but his credibility was shattered. One by one, major Persian capitals fell: Babylon welcomed Alexander with little resistance; Susa handed over the royal treasure; and Persepolis—the ceremonial heart of the empire—awaited a similar fate.

The Burning of Persepolis

Alexander entered Persepolis in early 330 BCE. Initially, he treated the city with respect. However, a few months later, a fire broke out that destroyed much of the grand palace complex. Ancient sources disagree on the cause: some say Alexander was drunk and set it ablaze in revenge for Xerxes's burning of Athens. Others suggest it was accidental or done as a political statement to show the end of Persian rule.

Regardless of the reason, the burning of Persepolis symbolized the final blow to the Achaemenid dynasty. The city's great palaces and artistic treasures were lost in the flames. Alexander took huge amounts of gold and silver from Persian treasuries, wealth that would fund his future campaigns and enrich his soldiers.

The Pursuit and Death of Darius III

Even after Gaugamela, Darius III was still alive, fleeing deeper into the eastern provinces. He hoped to raise an army among the Bactrians or other peoples in Central Asia. But many of his own satraps doubted he could turn the situation around. One such satrap, **Bessus**, decided to take matters into his own hands.

As Alexander's forces closed in, Bessus and a group of conspirators arrested Darius. They hoped to set up Bessus as the new king under the name **Artaxerxes V**. But before Alexander could rescue Darius,

Bessus's men stabbed him, leaving him to die in a wagon by the roadside. When Alexander found the wounded Darius, he reportedly gave him water and promised to avenge his murder. Darius died soon after, ending the official lineage of Achaemenid kings.

Alexander then declared himself the rightful successor to Darius. He pursued Bessus, capturing him later in Central Asia. Alexander handed Bessus over to Persian nobles for punishment, claiming to uphold Persian law and honor Darius's memory.

Alexander's Rule over Former Persian Lands

With Darius III dead, most of the empire recognized Alexander as king. However, some eastern regions continued to resist. Alexander spent several years pacifying Bactria and Sogdiana (parts of modern Central Asia). He married Roxana, a local princess, to win support among the high families there.

Alexander also adopted Persian customs at his court, including the practice of **proskynesis**, where subjects bowed to the king. Many Macedonians disliked these Persian traditions, feeling they went against Greek ideals of equality among free men. But Alexander wanted to unify the empire by blending Greek and Persian cultures, hoping to be accepted by all his subjects.

The End of the Achaemenid Empire

Though small pockets of resistance remained, the Achaemenid Empire as a ruling power ended with Darius III's death in 330 BCE. Alexander continued to push east, reaching the edges of India before his army, worn out by years of campaigning, demanded to return home. Along the way, he founded multiple cities named **Alexandria**, spreading Greek culture across the former Persian lands.

Under Alexander's rule, the old Persian satrapies became provinces of his empire, governed by Macedonian or Greek officers, often alongside local Persian nobles. He kept many Persian administrative practices, such as using existing tax systems and roads, because they were highly efficient. This combination of Greek and Persian ways is sometimes called the **Hellenistic** world, where Greek language and art blended with local traditions.

Alexander's Death and the Aftermath

In 323 BCE, after returning to Babylon, Alexander died suddenly—likely from fever, though some suspect other causes. Because he left no clear adult heir, his generals—known as the **Diadochi**—fought over control of the vast territories he had conquered.

Eventually, Alexander's empire broke into several smaller kingdoms. In the east, one of these was the **Seleucid Empire**, founded by Seleucus I Nicator, which included much of the old Persian lands. Although the Achaemenid line had ended, many Persian customs and systems lived on under the Seleucids and later dynasties.

For the Persian people, Alexander's invasion was a moment of great change. Some embraced the blend of Greek and Persian cultures. Others remembered the glory days of Cyrus, Darius I, and Xerxes with sadness. Over time, new Iranian dynasties would rise—such as the Parthians and the Sasanians—and claim to restore the spirit of ancient Persia.

Reflections on the Achaemenid Legacy

The fall of the Achaemenid Empire in 330 BCE did not erase its influence. The Achaemenids created a model of governance that blended respect for local cultures with a powerful central king. Their road systems, coinage, and satrapy administration left a strong mark on the lands they once ruled. Even Alexander admired and borrowed many Persian ideas, hoping to keep the empire running smoothly under his command.

Persian art, architecture, and religious practices also left a deep imprint. The monumental palaces at places like Persepolis, even in ruins, inspired future generations. The empire's tradition of tolerance for different faiths, languages, and customs showed a different path than harsh conquerors like the Assyrians had taken centuries before.

Though the empire ended with Darius III, the Persian people continued their rich cultural heritage. New rulers would come and go, but the memory of Cyrus the Great's vision and Darius I's administrative genius would survive in legends, stories, and physical remains across Iran and beyond.

Conclusion of Chapter 8

Alexander the Great's swift conquest brought an end to the Achaemenid Empire, one of the largest and most influential empires of the ancient world. In a series of major battles—Granicus, Issus, and Gaugamela—he defeated Darius III, eventually capturing the Persian heartlands and burning Persepolis. With Darius's murder, Alexander claimed the Persian throne, uniting Greek and Persian traditions under his rule.

This moment reshaped the political map of the ancient world. Where once Persian kings ruled from the Aegean Sea to the Indus Valley, Alexander's empire now rose. But Alexander's death soon divided that empire among his generals, leading to new kingdoms and changing alliances. Yet the Achaemenid legacy remained. Their style of governance, their respect for different cultures, and their impressive building projects influenced the centuries that followed.

CHAPTER 9

THE SELEUCID PERIOD

Introduction

In our last chapters, we saw how Alexander the Great conquered the Persian Empire. After Alexander's sudden death in 323 BCE, his generals—often called the "Diadochi"—fought among themselves for control of the huge realm he left behind. Out of these struggles rose several Hellenistic kingdoms. One of them was the **Seleucid Empire**, which took over much of the old Achaemenid lands in Asia, including most of Iran.

In this chapter, we will explore what happened in Persia under Seleucid rule. We will see how the Seleucid kings tried to keep a diverse empire together by blending Greek customs with local traditions. We will learn about the difficulties they faced: powerful rivals, ongoing revolts, and a constantly shifting political landscape. We will also discover how local Iranian peoples, such as those in Parthia, started to break away, leading to the Seleucids' gradual loss of power in the region. By the end, we will see the stage set for the rise of the Parthians, who would become the new masters of the Iranian Plateau.

The Aftermath of Alexander's Death

When Alexander died in Babylon (323 BCE), he left no strong adult heir. His half-brother Arrhidaeus (Philip III) and his infant son Alexander IV were declared kings in name, but real control fell to

Alexander's top generals. Over the next few decades, these generals fought each other in a series of conflicts called the **Wars of the Diadochi**.

- **Ptolemy** took Egypt.
- **Antigonus** held parts of Asia Minor and the Levant for a time.
- **Cassander** controlled Macedonia and parts of Greece.
- **Lysimachus** eventually ruled Thrace and western Asia Minor.
- **Seleucus I Nicator** ended up dominating a vast area stretching from Syria to parts of Central Asia.

It was Seleucus I (Seleucus "the Victor") who founded the Seleucid Empire. Through battle and negotiation, he took possession of most of Alexander's lands in the east, including Mesopotamia, Persia (Iran), and even regions further east. His empire, at its height, reached from parts of modern-day Turkey to parts of present-day Afghanistan.

Founding the Seleucid Empire

Seleucus I Nicator started as a general under Alexander. After many power struggles, by around 305 BCE he claimed the title of king. He made a capital in **Babylon** first, then built or expanded cities such as **Seleucia on the Tigris**. Later, he also founded **Antioch** on the Orontes River (in present-day Turkey/Syria region), which became another important capital.

For a short time, Seleucus cooperated with Lysimachus and other Diadochi. But alliances shifted quickly. In 281 BCE, Seleucus defeated Lysimachus in battle. Now he was the strongest ruler in Asia, controlling land that included large parts of the old Persian heartland. However, Seleucus was assassinated the next year (280 BCE), leaving his son, **Antiochus I Soter**, to inherit a massive but fragile empire.

From the start, the Seleucid kings faced a huge challenge: they were Greek-speaking rulers trying to control many lands with different languages, religions, and traditions. In the Iranian Plateau, most people still followed local customs and had little desire to adopt Greek ways. The Seleucids tried to found Greek-style cities and encourage Greek settlers to move east, hoping to form a ruling class loyal to them. But this policy met with mixed success.

Life in the Seleucid East: Blending Cultures

The Seleucids introduced Hellenistic culture to Asia. In major cities, you might find Greek theaters, gymnasiums, and marketplaces. Some local nobles learned Greek to deal with the royal court, and some even sent their children to Greek schools. Greek coins were minted with the king's portrait. Art and architecture showed Greek styles mixed with Mesopotamian and Iranian influences.

At the same time, the Seleucids recognized the need to respect local customs. They allowed some regions to keep their religious practices, temples, and local laws. In older Achaemenid capitals like **Susa** and **Ecbatana**, local elites kept some power. In fact, the Seleucid kings often used the Achaemenid system of **satrapies**. They appointed satraps (governors) to collect taxes and maintain order.

Yet there was a difference: many Seleucid-appointed satraps were Greek or Macedonian, especially in the western parts of the empire. Over time, some Iranians, Babylonians, and others rose in the Seleucid administration, but high positions often remained with Greeks. This caused resentment in places where local people felt sidelined by foreign rulers.

Antiochus I, Antiochus II, and Early Challenges

Antiochus I Soter (reigned 281–261 BCE) inherited his father's vast territories but also many struggles. He faced attacks from other Hellenistic rulers, including Ptolemy II in Egypt, who wanted to grab parts of the Levant. He also dealt with unrest in the eastern provinces. Antiochus I managed to defend his core lands in Mesopotamia and Syria, but he lost some ground in Asia Minor to rival kings.

Antiochus II Theos (reigned 261–246 BCE) continued fighting with the Ptolemies in a series of conflicts called the **Syrian Wars**. These wars drained the empire's resources. Also, eastern satrapies like Bactria and Parthia began slipping from central control. Local governors sensed the Seleucids were too busy fighting in the west to pay attention.

During this time, some Greek communities in the eastern provinces grew wealthy through trade. Caravan routes connected the Seleucid lands to Central Asia, India, and beyond. However, the empire was stretched thin. The kings had to rely on local rulers to keep order. If a local governor decided to rebel or declare independence, it was not easy for Antiochus II to send a big army all the way from Syria to the far east.

The Growth of Hellenistic Cities in Iran

In parts of Iran, especially near important trade routes, Seleucid kings or local rulers founded cities with Greek-style institutions. These included places like **Seleucia on the Eulaeus** near Susa, **Alexandria in Susiana**, or refounded older towns with Greek names. The goal was to settle Greek colonists who would be loyal to the king and bring Hellenistic culture.

In these cities, one might see a blend of Greek and Iranian traditions. Some people worshipped Greek gods, while others continued to honor Iranian deities like Anahita or Mithra. Sculptures might show Greek poses but include local clothing or symbols. Over time, a new mixed culture evolved, at least in the cities. In rural areas, most people carried on with their traditional farming, crafts, and local beliefs, seeing little need to adopt foreign customs.

For the Seleucids, having these Greek-style cities was a way to project power. If revolts broke out, they could rely on the loyalty of Greek settlers. These towns also became trading hubs, connecting the region's wealth—spices, textiles, metals—to markets further west. But as we will see, this was not enough to hold the empire together when stronger local dynasties arose.

The Breakaway of Bactria and Parthia

A major blow to Seleucid control happened when some eastern satraps decided to form their own kingdoms. The best-known examples are **Bactria** and **Parthia**.

1. **Bactria**: The region south of the Oxus River (modern Amu Darya), centered on the city of **Bactra** (Balkh), was rich in farmland and a crossroads for trade with India and China. Around 250 BCE, the local satrap **Diodotus** declared independence from the Seleucids. He set up the **Greco-Bactrian Kingdom**, which became quite powerful and wealthy.
2. **Parthia**: In the same period, a man named **Andragoras** was the Seleucid governor of Parthia (northeastern Iran). But a group called the **Parni**—led by **Arsaces**—invaded and took Parthia from Andragoras. This event marked the birth of the **Parthian Empire** under the **Arsacid Dynasty**.

These breakaways showed that the Seleucid Empire was losing its grip. The kings tried to reconquer Bactria and Parthia, but they were distracted by wars in the west. Each time they turned attention east, new troubles in Asia Minor or Syria pulled them back. Over time, Bactria and Parthia grew stronger, while the Seleucids weakened.

The Reign of Antiochus III (223-187 BCE): A Revival Attempt

Antiochus III (often called "the Great") came to the throne as a young man. He hoped to restore the empire to its old glory. Early in his reign, he faced rebellions and lost territory. But step by step, Antiochus III rebuilt the Seleucid army and recaptured many lands.

1. **Campaigns in the East**: Antiochus III marched through Iran, reasserting control over rebellious satrapies. He retook parts of Parthia and Bactria, forcing local rulers to accept his authority—at least on paper. This is sometimes called his **Anabasis**, a term borrowed from Greek meaning a "march inland."

2. **Success Against Egypt**: Antiochus III also fought against the Ptolemaic Kingdom of Egypt (another Greek dynasty) in what historians call the **Fifth Syrian War** (202–195 BCE). He succeeded in capturing much of Coele-Syria (modern Syria-Lebanon area), giving the Seleucids more secure control of the region.
3. **Conflict with Rome**: Antiochus III then turned to the Aegean Sea, hoping to extend his influence there. But he ran into the rising power of **Rome**, which had already defeated Carthage in the west. Roman legions clashed with Antiochus III's forces in Asia Minor and Greece. In the **Battle of Magnesia** (190 BCE), the Romans decisively beat the Seleucids. This defeat forced Antiochus III to pay heavy tribute to Rome and give up most claims in Asia Minor. He was later killed in an eastern campaign, leaving a weakened empire to his successors.

Though Antiochus III briefly restored Seleucid power in Iran, it did not last. The empire's structure remained fragile. Local rulers kept pushing for independence, and the strain of constant wars wore down the royal treasury.

Rome, Internal Struggles, and Decline

After Antiochus III, the Seleucid Empire faced continuous problems. **Seleucus IV** (187–175 BCE) tried to manage finances and pay Rome's demands, but his rule was short. **Antiochus IV Epiphanes** (175–164 BCE) became famous for his conflicts with the Jewish people in Judea and for building grand projects in Syria. He temporarily regained some strength for the empire but then got entangled in more wars.

As time went on, Rome kept a close eye on the Seleucids. Roman ambassadors interfered in local affairs, ensuring the Seleucid kings did not grow too strong again. Meanwhile, the Parthians expanded in Iran, taking over more land. By the late second century BCE, the Seleucids were little more than a local power in Syria and parts of Mesopotamia. Their once-vast territories in Iran were mostly gone, either controlled by Parthia or by small local dynasties.

Civil wars among Seleucid princes made things worse. Rival claimants to the throne called on foreign powers—like the Parthians or the Romans—for help, further weakening central authority. Gradually, the empire shrank to a small region around Antioch in Syria.

Cultural Influence of the Seleucids in Persia

Even though the Seleucids lost direct control over large parts of Iran, their cultural impact remained. In some cities, Greek language and art styles continued to be used for generations. Local rulers who succeeded the Seleucids often adopted Greek titles or coin designs. Trade routes that the Seleucids promoted stayed busy, connecting the Mediterranean world with Central Asia.

In religion, there was also some blending. Greek gods like Zeus and Apollo were sometimes worshipped alongside Iranian gods like Mithra or Anahita. Philosophical ideas from Greece may have reached local Iranian elites, while Iranian spiritual beliefs also traveled westward. This period of cultural mixing set the stage for later empires, like the Parthians and Sasanians, to absorb and adapt Hellenistic influences in their own ways.

But for most Iranians living in villages or small towns, life probably did not change too much. They still spoke their local languages, observed their traditional customs, and paid taxes to whoever claimed to be in charge that year—whether that was a Seleucid governor, a rogue satrap, or an up-and-coming Parthian chief.

Late Seleucid Struggles

By the middle of the second century BCE, **Parthia** was growing stronger under kings like **Mithridates I** (reigned c. 171–138 BCE). The Parthians moved westward, seizing Media and other parts of Iran from the Seleucids. In 141 BCE, they even captured the city of Seleucia on the Tigris. This was a massive loss for the Seleucid crown.

Though some Seleucid rulers tried to strike back, the empire was no longer in a position to put together a serious campaign in the east. Even in the west, they faced challenges from local dynasties and the expanding Roman Republic. The Seleucid kings changed frequently, often due to assassinations or civil wars.

One last attempt to fight back in the east was made by **Antiochus VII Sidetes** (reigned 138–129 BCE). He led a campaign against the Parthians and briefly recaptured parts of Mesopotamia and Babylonia. However, he was killed in battle against the Parthians in 129 BCE, ending any real chance of Seleucid revival in Iran.

The Final Chapter of the Seleucids

After Antiochus VII's death, the Seleucid "empire" became a small Syrian kingdom. Kings such as **Demetrius II**, **Antiochus VIII**, and **Antiochus IX** fought each other, Roman influence grew, and local leaders carved out their own fiefdoms. In 64 BCE, the Roman general Pompey turned what was left of the Seleucid realm into a Roman province called **Syria**.

By this time, the old Achaemenid heartlands were firmly under Parthian rule. Hellenistic culture remained in pockets, but the kings who wore the crowns in the Iranian Plateau now belonged to the **Arsacid** (Parthian) dynasty. The Seleucid era in Persia was over.

Conclusion of Chapter 9

The Seleucid Empire arose from the chaos following Alexander the Great's death. At its peak, it stretched across a large portion of the ancient Near East, including the Iranian Plateau. Seleucid kings introduced Greek culture, built Greek-style cities, and tried to blend Hellenistic and local traditions. For a time, they held onto much of Alexander's eastern legacy.

But the empire was always fragile. Constant wars with rival Hellenistic states (like the Ptolemies of Egypt), interference from powerful Rome, and the independence movements of eastern satrapies all took their toll. Over time, regions like Bactria and Parthia broke away. The Seleucids never managed to fully reassert their power in Iran after these lands slipped from their grip.

CHAPTER 10

THE RISE OF THE PARTHIAN EMPIRE

Introduction

As the Seleucid Empire weakened, new powers rose to take its place in the Iranian lands. The most important of these was **Parthia**, ruled by the **Arsacid Dynasty**. The Parthians began as a small group of tribes in northeastern Iran but grew into a strong empire that controlled a huge region, from Mesopotamia to parts of Central Asia.

In this chapter, we will see how the Parthians emerged from under Seleucid rule. We will learn about the early Arsacid kings, like **Arsaces I**, and how they expanded their realm. We will discover the tactics that made Parthian armies so feared, including their skilled horse archers and heavy cavalry known as cataphracts. We will also meet the Parthian king **Mithridates I**, who truly transformed Parthia into a great empire. Finally, we will see how the Parthians managed their kingdom, balanced local traditions with Hellenistic influences, and set the stage for centuries of rivalry with Rome—just as the Achaemenids once faced off against Greece.

The Origins of the Parni and the Founding of Parthia

Parthia was originally a region in northeastern Iran, known for its mountains and semi-desert plains. Under the Achaemenids, it was a satrapy. Later, under the Seleucids, it was ruled by governors who might be Greek or local. The people living there included various Iranian tribes, one of which was called the **Parni**.

Around 250 BCE, a Parthian governor named **Andragoras** declared independence from the Seleucids. Soon after, **Arsaces**, leader of the Parni tribe, rebelled against Andragoras and took over Parthia, establishing the **Arsacid Dynasty**. Arsaces became the first Parthian king, though the exact date of his rule is unclear. Some historians place the start of his reign around 247 BCE, which is often used as the founding date of the Parthian Empire.

At first, the Parthian state was small and had to fight for survival. The Seleucids, busy with other conflicts, did not fully focus on crushing Parthia. This gave Arsaces and his successors time to build alliances, train troops, and fortify their homeland. They also learned from neighboring cultures. For example, they adopted some Greek administrative ideas but combined them with older Iranian traditions.

Arsaces and the Early Arsacid Kings

The early Parthian rulers carried the name "Arsaces" to honor their founding ancestor. After Arsaces I, his successors continued to strengthen Parthia, pushing back against Seleucid attempts to reconquer the region. They built fortresses, trained cavalry units, and made use of the region's rough terrain to defend themselves.

One reason the Parthians were so successful was their emphasis on **cavalry warfare**. Living in or near steppe lands, they learned horse-riding and archery from an early age. Their horsemen could shoot arrows with great accuracy while galloping away—this tactic became famous as the "Parthian shot." This mobility allowed smaller Parthian forces to defeat larger, slower Greek-style armies in open battles.

The Parthians also used heavy cavalry known as **cataphracts**. These armored riders wore metal scales or plates, and their horses were often armored too. Cataphracts could charge enemy lines with powerful shock attacks. Together, the light horse archers and heavy cataphracts made the Parthian army a flexible and dangerous force.

The Growth of Parthia Under Mithridates I

While earlier Arsacid kings laid the foundation, it was **Mithridates I** (reigned about 171–138 BCE) who truly expanded Parthia into a major empire. He took advantage of the Seleucid Empire's weakness under kings like Demetrius II. One by one, Mithridates I conquered neighboring regions:

1. **Media**: A region in northwestern Iran, centered on Ecbatana (modern Hamadan). Capturing Media gave Parthia a more strategic location and access to trade routes.
2. **Babylonia**: After defeating Seleucid forces, Mithridates I seized control of Mesopotamia and the famous city of Babylon. This was a big deal because Mesopotamia was rich in farmland and full of important trade centers.
3. **Elam**: He also pushed south toward Elam (near Susa), though details are less clear.

By the end of Mithridates I's reign, Parthia ruled a huge swath of land that included modern Iran, Iraq, and parts of surrounding areas. The Seleucids tried to strike back, but they were bogged down by wars in other regions. Also, Rome was growing more interested in the eastern Mediterranean, further distracting the Seleucids.

Mithridates I used a mix of force and diplomacy. He allowed local nobles to keep some power if they accepted Parthian rule. He struck coins that showed both Iranian and Greek influences, reflecting the mixed culture of his empire. By the time he died, Parthia had gone from a small rebellious province to the leading power in the eastern lands once held by Alexander's successors.

Administrative Methods and Cultural Policies

Like the Achaemenids before them, the Parthians did not force a single culture on their diverse population. They followed a loose system where local rulers (often called **vassal kings**) or powerful noble families governed various regions. In many areas, Greek city-states that had been founded by the Seleucids were allowed to keep their councils and Greek laws, as long as they recognized Parthian overlords and paid taxes.

In return, the Parthians demanded loyalty and military support in times of war. The Arsacid kings did not build a tightly centralized empire like Darius I had done. Instead, they let local powers run their own affairs, stepping in mainly to collect taxes or to settle major disputes. This approach kept administration simpler, but it also meant the Parthian Empire could be fragile when strong central leadership was missing.

Because Greek influence was still present, especially in major cities, Hellenistic culture continued to mingle with Iranian traditions. We see this in coin designs, where Parthian kings often wore Iranian headdresses but printed Greek legends (inscriptions) around the edges. Over time, the Parthians also revived older Iranian customs, such as the worship of deities like Mithra. They built fire temples in some regions, showing a link to ancient Iranian religious ideas (pre-Zoroastrian or related to it).

Conflict with the Seleucids and Expansion West

As Parthia grew, it clashed with the Seleucids in Mesopotamia. One of the pivotal conflicts came during the reign of **Phraates II** (son of Mithridates I). The Seleucid king **Antiochus VII Sidetes** launched a major campaign to reclaim the east. He scored some victories, retaking parts of Mesopotamia. However, Phraates II managed to defeat and kill Antiochus VII in 129 BCE.

This victory effectively ended Seleucid power in the Iranian Plateau and Babylonian regions. From then on, the Parthians were the main force in those lands. Now, only local dynasties or smaller Greek-ruled states, like the Greco-Bactrian Kingdom, remained in the far east. Over time, Parthia even exerted influence over sections of Armenia and other nearby regions.

But as the Parthians moved farther west, they came into contact with the expanding Roman Republic. Rome, having conquered much of the Mediterranean, saw Mesopotamia and parts of the Near East as valuable areas to influence or control. This set up the next big rivalry in the region: Parthia vs. Rome.

Parthian Society and Nobility

A key feature of the Parthian system was the power of the **nobility**, also called the "Seven Great Houses" in some later traditions. These noble families had their own armies, estates, and local rule. The king needed their support to stay on the throne. If a king was weak or unpopular, nobles could rebel or replace him with another Arsacid prince.

This meant the Parthian king had to keep the nobility happy, often by granting them privileges or marrying into their families. The empire was, in some ways, a confederation of powerful noble clans under the leadership of the Arsacid house. At times, this arrangement helped the empire endure because local nobles defended their own lands fiercely. However, it also led to internal strife when nobles disagreed or plotted against the royal court.

Parthian Military Strength

The Parthian army's most famous tactic was the combination of fast horse archers and heavily armored cavalry. On the battlefield, Parthian horse archers would harass enemy formations, firing arrows even while retreating. If the enemy chased them, the cataphracts could charge in, using their weight to break through.

The Parthians learned from earlier Iranian cavalry traditions (such as the Scythians and older Achaemenid practices) and refined them. Unlike the Greek phalanx, which relied on tight infantry formations with long spears, the Parthians preferred mobile engagements where their cavalry could avoid direct confrontation until the moment was right.

Because of this style, the Parthians often avoided pitched battles in open fields if the enemy had strong infantry. Instead, they tried to lure opponents into deserts or steppe country, where the Parthian horsemen had the advantage. This approach would prove very effective against Roman armies later on, most famously at the **Battle of Carrhae** in 53 BCE.

Culture and Art in the Early Parthian Period

Parthian culture was a blend of Iranian, Hellenistic, and local Mesopotamian influences:

- **Sculpture**: Parthian art showed realistic human figures, sometimes wearing Greek garments and sometimes Iranian robes and trousers. Statues and reliefs in places like Hatra or on rock faces in Iran often had a mix of styles.
- **Coins**: Early Parthian coins used Greek letters with pictures of kings on one side and Greek gods or symbols on the other. Over time, some coins began to show more Iranian motifs, like the use of a seated archer or references to local deities.
- **Religion**: People in Parthian lands followed many faiths: Greek pantheons in some cities, local Mesopotamian gods in Babylon, Iranian deities in rural areas, and even early forms of Zoroastrianism. The Parthian kings did not impose one official religion, but they often showed favor to Iranian traditions, connecting themselves to old royal customs.

- **Language**: Greek remained important for administration and diplomacy, especially early on. Aramaic was also widely used as a common language for trade. Over time, Middle Persian or Parthian dialects gained ground at court, reflecting the empire's Iranian identity.

Rivalries and Internal Strife

The Parthian system worked best when a strong king like Mithridates I was in charge. But after his death, there were frequent struggles over the throne. Some kings ruled only a few years before being dethroned or killed. The powerful nobles, each commanding their own armies, often decided who would be recognized as "Great King." This made the Parthian royal court a place of intrigue and shifting alliances.

These internal disputes sometimes led to breakaway provinces or local dynasties that acted independently. Still, the Parthians held onto the key centers of power in Iran and Mesopotamia. They maintained the Silk Road trade route, which passed through their territory, connecting East Asia to the Mediterranean. Caravans carried silk, spices, metals, glassware, and other valuables, bringing wealth to Parthian lands.

This trade helped the Parthians finance their armies and keep local elites loyal, as everyone profited from the flow of goods. The empire's central position between Rome in the west and Han China in the east gave it economic importance, even if its political structure was not as centralized as earlier or later Persian empires.

Mithridates II and the Height of Parthian Power

Mithridates II (sometimes called Mithridates the Great, reigned c. 124–88 BCE) is considered one of the most successful Parthian rulers after Mithridates I. He reorganized the empire, dealt with threats from the Scythians or other nomadic peoples in the northeast, and extended Parthian influence west into Armenia and parts of Mesopotamia.

Mithridates II also established the first direct contacts between Parthia and Rome. Around 92 BCE, Roman legates met with the Parthian court to discuss trade and possibly alliances against common enemies. Although the two powers would later become fierce rivals, this first meeting showed that Parthia was recognized as a major state by Rome.

During Mithridates II's reign, the empire was quite stable and wealthy. His coins bore grand titles, reflecting confidence and power. He improved the roads and maintained cities that were key stops along the trade routes. Even though there were always local tensions and border conflicts, Parthia under Mithridates II rivaled the old glories of the Achaemenids in terms of land area and influence—though it was governed in a more decentralized way.

Relations with Neighboring Kingdoms

Beyond dealing with the fading Seleucids, the Parthians also had complex relations with:

- **Armenia**: Sometimes an ally, sometimes a rival. Armenian kings like Tigranes the Great built their own empire, which overlapped with Parthian interests in Mesopotamia.

- **Bactria**: The Greco-Bactrian Kingdom eventually broke into smaller states, some of which became the Indo-Greek kingdoms in what is now Afghanistan and northern India. Parthia sometimes fought them but mostly focused on western expansion.
- **Scythians/Sakas**: Nomadic groups from Central Asia who occasionally raided Parthian lands or joined alliances with or against the Parthians.

Managing these neighbors required skillful diplomacy. The Parthians could marry into Armenian or other royal families to form alliances. They could also support rival claimants to local thrones, using them as puppets. These tactics mirrored the old Achaemenid and Seleucid methods of controlling border regions without direct occupation.

The Early Struggles with Rome

Although the Parthians first met with Rome peacefully under Mithridates II, tensions soon rose. Rome's power extended deep into Asia Minor and the Levant. The Roman general Pompey rearranged the politics of the Near East in the mid-first century BCE, toppling kingdoms that opposed him. Parthia watched these events carefully.

One of Rome's triumvirs, **Marcus Licinius Crassus**, invaded Parthian territory in 53 BCE, seeking glory and wealth. He marched into Mesopotamia with a large Roman army but was defeated at the **Battle of Carrhae**, where Parthian horse archers and cataphracts proved deadly. Crassus himself was killed, and tens of thousands of Roman soldiers were captured or killed. This shocking loss for Rome marked Parthia as a formidable power.

However, this major defeat at Carrhae also sparked a long cycle of wars and uneasy truces between Rome and Parthia. The eastern frontier became a zone of conflict where each side tried to outmaneuver the other by using local allies, launching raids, or placing friendly rulers on local thrones. Future chapters will explore these Roman-Parthian battles in more detail, showing how the two empires struggled for dominance in the Near East.

CHAPTER 11

THE HEIGHT OF PARTHIAN POWER

Introduction

In the previous chapters, we learned how the Parthians rose from a small group in northeastern Iran to become the main power in the old Seleucid lands. Under early kings like Arsaces I and Mithridates I, they took control of large parts of Iran and Mesopotamia, replacing the weakened Seleucid Empire. Parthian armies used swift horse archers and heavily armored cavalry to defeat bigger foes, including the Seleucids and even the Romans at the Battle of Carrhae (53 BCE).

Now, we move into a time often called the "Height of Parthian Power." This period stretched from around the middle of the 1st century BCE to the early 1st century CE. During these decades, Parthian kings secured their hold on Mesopotamia, built alliances or fought with Rome depending on circumstances, and expanded trade along the Silk Road. Their capital cities—like Ctesiphon—grew into important cultural centers. Yet this success did not come easily. Internal struggles among nobles and rival claimants to the throne challenged the stability of the empire, forcing Parthian kings to balance powerful noble families against the need for central authority.

In this chapter, we explore how the Parthians reached their greatest extent, how they governed so many lands with different peoples, and how they interacted with Rome in both war and diplomacy. We will examine the reigns of notable Parthian rulers such as Orodes II and Phraates IV, as well as the complex relationships between the royal court, local nobility, and neighboring powers. Finally, we will take a closer look at Parthian culture at its peak—how they blended Iranian traditions with Hellenistic and Mesopotamian elements, how trade routes flourished, and how the empire adapted to constant change.

---

1. After Carrhae: Parthian Confidence and Challenges

The Parthian victory over the Roman general Crassus at Carrhae in 53 BCE was a major milestone. It showed that Rome, which had become the most powerful force around the Mediterranean, could be defeated in the East. Parthian king **Orodes II** (reigned c. 57–37 BCE) gained tremendous prestige from this success, and he and his nobles felt that their empire was the undisputed champion of the region.

However, triumph sometimes brings new challenges. The Parthian nobility had seen that a well-led Parthian army could outfight even a famous Roman one. This further empowered some of the great noble houses. They believed that the monarchy depended on their cavalry forces to win. As a result, some nobles demanded greater autonomy or influence in the royal court. Also, Rome was down but not destroyed. In fact, Roman politics soon shifted, and new leaders would rise—like Julius Caesar and Mark Antony—who might try to avenge Crassus's defeat.

In addition, the **Roman Civil Wars** (49–31 BCE) began to unfold in the west. Julius Caesar fought Pompey, then later Mark Antony and Octavian (the future Emperor Augustus) struggled for power. Parthia found opportunities in these wars to expand its influence, but it also risked being drawn into Roman affairs in ways that could backfire if the wrong side won. Orodes II, therefore, had to weigh each choice carefully while also managing tensions at home, among his own nobles and family.

2. Orodes II's Reign and Its Ups and Downs

Orodes II was a skilled politician who knew how to take advantage of Rome's distractions. Right after Carrhae, he celebrated the victory by having the Roman general Crassus's captured standards displayed as trophies. One of his top military leaders, known as **Surena**, had played a key role in that battle, but Surena's popularity made Orodes II uneasy. Fearing Surena's power, Orodes II had him executed soon after. This was a sign that internal court politics were treacherous: successful generals could overshadow the king if not managed.

Alliance with Pompey's Son

During the Roman Civil War between Julius Caesar and Pompey, Orodes II offered help to Pompey's surviving son, who was seeking allies. Orodes hoped that by supporting a weaker Roman faction, he could keep Rome divided and out of the East. However, Caesar eventually became the dominant figure in Rome before his assassination in 44 BCE, leaving Parthia unsure where to stand next.

Pacorus I and the Invasion of Roman Syria

One of Orodes II's sons, **Pacorus I**, led a major campaign into Roman territory around 40 BCE. The Parthians, with help from local anti-Roman groups, seized large portions of Syria and even advanced into parts of Asia Minor. For a brief moment, it seemed Parthia could permanently take over these western regions. But the Roman general **Ventidius** rallied Roman forces, defeated Pacorus in 38 BCE, and killed him in battle. This blow devastated Orodes II, who had lost his heir. Overcome by grief and perhaps seeing weakness in the monarchy, Orodes's other sons turned on him. In the end, Orodes II was murdered by one of his sons, **Phraates IV**, around 37 BCE.

Orodes II's rule had brought both high achievements (Carrhae) and setbacks (the loss of Pacorus and the campaign in Syria). The constant tension between using powerful nobles to wage war and controlling them at home remained a central issue. Now, Phraates IV ascended the throne, inheriting a strong empire still proud of its military might—but also haunted by family plots and Roman threats.

---

3. Phraates IV and the Search for Stability

Phraates IV (reigned c. 37–2 BCE) came to power by killing his father, Orodes II, and several of his own brothers to remove any competition for the throne. This harsh beginning showed that palace intrigue in Parthia was as dangerous as ever. Ruling a large empire meant balancing the demands of nobles, protecting borders from nomadic tribes in the east, and dealing with Rome in the west.

Relations with Mark Antony

While Phraates IV secured his throne, Rome fell under the joint leadership of Mark Antony and Octavian (later Emperor Augustus). Mark Antony took control of Rome's eastern provinces and prepared a grand campaign to avenge Crassus's defeat. In 36 BCE, he led a big army into Parthian lands, hoping to repeat Alexander the Great's success and win personal glory.

Antony's campaign started badly. He faced supply problems and fierce Parthian cavalry attacks. In a series of skirmishes, Parthian horse archers harassed Roman columns, forcing them into slow retreats. Winter weather added to Antony's troubles. By the end, he lost a large part of his army to battle, disease, and desertion. Antony retreated back to Roman Syria, accomplishing little beyond more bloodshed. These events increased Phraates IV's reputation, but the Parthian king still had to manage court affairs carefully. Some nobles might grow jealous of a successful king. Others might question the violence Phraates used to claim power.

Internal Revolts and Phraates' Paranoia

Because Phraates IV had come to power through violence, many within the royal family hated him. He feared plots by cousins, half-brothers, or even wives and concubines. The powerful noble houses sometimes backed rival claimants if they thought it would help them gain land or privileges. Phraates responded with even more cruelty, executing any relative who seemed disloyal.

A major turning point came when a rebellion forced Phraates IV to flee briefly. He had to call on nomadic Scythian tribes for help. Once he regained the throne, he rewarded these tribes with gifts and land, further upsetting some local elites. This back-and-forth struggle shows how unstable the Parthian crown could be without a stable process of succession.

Deal with Augustus and Return of the Eagles

Meanwhile, Mark Antony was defeated in his civil war against Octavian. By 31 BCE, Octavian emerged as the unchallenged ruler of Rome, taking the name **Augustus** in 27 BCE. Augustus wished for peace in the East so he could focus on reorganizing the empire. Phraates IV, still wary of Roman invasions, was also open to an agreement.

In 20 BCE, Augustus and Phraates IV reached a historic deal: the Parthians returned the legionary standards captured at Carrhae decades earlier, along with some prisoners. In return, Rome recognized Parthia's control over certain lands east of the Euphrates and stayed out of a direct war. Augustus celebrated this as a diplomatic victory—the standards, precious to Roman pride, were returned without another costly war. For Parthia, the arrangement guaranteed some breathing room to handle internal issues without fear of immediate Roman invasion.

This peace helped Phraates IV stabilize his reign at least on the western frontier. Yet friction remained. The Euphrates River became the unofficial boundary between the Roman and Parthian spheres of influence, though local rulers in places like Armenia and Syria could still cause tension by switching loyalties.

---

4. The Parthian Court and Society at Its Peak

By the late 1st century BCE, Parthia stood near its greatest territorial extent. It controlled Iran, Mesopotamia, and had influence over neighboring regions like Armenia. The capital area near **Ctesiphon**—an area located across the Tigris from the old city of Seleucia—was becoming the main political center, though royal courts also traveled to older capitals like Ecbatana (Hamadan) and even spent time in Babylon for ceremonial events.

Court Life and the King's Authority

The Parthian king was surrounded by court officials, nobles, and family members who each had their own agendas. A council of noblemen and senior courtiers, sometimes called the **Megistanes**, advised (or pressured) the king. Major decisions—like declaring war or selecting heirs—often required noble support. If the king lost favor with the Megistanes, they could back a different prince from the Arsacid family, igniting a civil war.

The king displayed his authority through lavish banquets, public ceremonies, and gift-giving. He gave out golden ornaments, fine horses, and land grants to loyal nobles. This generosity fostered loyalty but could also stir envy among those who felt overlooked. Royal weddings were especially important political events, as the king might marry daughters of powerful noble families or local dynasties. By tying these families to the crown, the king hoped to keep them from rebelling.

Nobles and Local Autonomy

Below the king, powerful noble houses owned large estates with peasants, horsemen, and craftsmen. Some had their own small forts or cities. They collected local taxes and kept local order, sometimes coining their own currency or maintaining private armies. As long as they paid tribute and answered the king's call for troops, they had considerable freedom. This system was very different from the centralized style of governance used by the old Achaemenids or by the Romans. It fit the Parthian mindset, which placed high value on aristocratic honor and personal loyalty.

However, this arrangement caused repeated tensions when certain noble families felt the king was ignoring their rights or favoring rivals. If one noble house grew too strong, the king might try to remove or weaken it, leading to conspiracies and revolt. Stable kings who ruled for many years (like Phraates IV, despite his troubles) needed to balance these interests skillfully.

---

5. Parthian Culture: Blending and Innovation

At the height of their power, the Parthians presided over a rich cultural fusion. They took parts of Greek, Mesopotamian, and older Iranian heritages and forged something unique.

- **Architecture**: Parthian buildings showed a mix of Greek column styles and Iranian courtyard layouts. Large halls with barrel vaults and iwans (arched doorways open on one side) appeared in some palaces, likely influencing later Islamic architecture.
- **Sculpture and Art**: Some Parthian statues looked stiff or frontal, a style different from Greek naturalism. Royal statues might show kings in long Iranian tunics, wearing the Parthian tiara or headdress, but still use Greek inscriptions around the base.

- **Religious Practices**: Different faiths coexisted. Zoroastrian traditions (like reverence for fire) appeared in some areas, though official Zoroastrianism might not have been as strictly organized as it later became. Temples to local Mesopotamian gods continued in cities like Babylon. Greek gods were honored in some old Seleucid-founded towns. Over time, many gods blended or were identified with each other.
- **Language**: Greek remained important for official documents in some regions, but Aramaic was widely used for day-to-day record keeping. Various Iranian dialects also thrived, especially in the countryside. By the 1st century CE, Parthian inscriptions began to appear in more places, showing a shift toward Iranian languages at the higher levels of administration.

Trade routes, known collectively as the **Silk Road**, connected Parthia to Central Asia, China, India, and the Roman world. Caravans carried silk, spices, metals, glass, and other valuables through Parthian territories, bringing wealth and ideas. This commerce allowed for cultural exchange, so towns in Parthia could have Greek theaters, Iranian religious sites, Mesopotamian temples, and visiting merchants from as far away as Rome or the Indus Valley.

---

6. Extending Influence: Armenia and Beyond

Armenia lay northwest of Parthia, between the Roman provinces in Asia Minor and the Parthian heartlands in Iran. Its kings often found themselves squeezed between Rome and Parthia. If an Armenian king leaned too far toward Rome, Parthia might invade; if he favored Parthia too openly, Rome would step in. This region became a constant flashpoint, with each empire trying to place friendly rulers on the Armenian throne.

The Case of Tigranes the Great (Earlier Period)

Earlier in the 1st century BCE, **Tigranes the Great** of Armenia built his own empire, at times allied with the Parthians and at other times fighting them. By the height of the Parthian era we are now discussing, Tigranes was gone, but the pattern remained: control of Armenia was a measure of prestige for both Rome and Parthia.

Diplomacy and Power Plays

Parthian kings recognized that a stable Armenia under a sympathetic king would keep Rome from pressing further east. They also did not want to directly occupy Armenia because that would provoke a major Roman response. So Parthia usually supported a local Armenian prince from the Arsacid family or a related dynasty, ensuring friendly ties.

The system could break down when that prince died or turned against Parthia, triggering Roman intervention. Thus, for much of Parthian history, Armenia served as a buffer region. Keeping it under indirect Parthian influence without pushing Rome into a full-scale war was a delicate game that required constant vigilance.

---

7. Rival Claimants and the Role of Rome

One major pattern of Parthian history involved rival claimants to the throne seeking Roman help. Or, in some cases, a Parthian noble rebelled and looked for backing from Rome. If the Roman Emperor (e.g., Augustus, Tiberius, or Nero) found it useful to weaken Parthia, he might support the challenger.

For instance, after Phraates IV died (around 2 BCE), there was a series of short-lived kings and power struggles. Some members of the Arsacid family fled to Roman territory, hoping to gain support for their return. The Romans, meanwhile, recognized that a divided Parthian kingdom was less dangerous, so they often played different Parthian princes off each other.

This external meddling contributed to cycles of civil war, especially when a strong king died without naming a clear successor. The next king had to spend precious resources fighting rivals instead of improving administration or defending against nomadic raids in the east. Still, the fundamental structure—king plus powerful noble houses—kept the empire together. No single noble house could overthrow the Arsacids entirely, and foreign invasions rarely penetrated deep except under extraordinary circumstances.

8. Succession of Parthian Kings in the Early 1st Century CE

Following Phraates IV, the early 1st century CE saw kings like **Phraataces (Phraates V)** and **Orodes III**. Their reigns were short and full of court intrigues. Eventually, **Vonones I**—a king raised in Rome—took the throne around 8 CE. Because Vonones was seen as too "Romanized," the Parthian nobility rejected him, replacing him with **Artabanus II**, a more traditionally Iranian-minded ruler.

Artabanus II (c. 10–38 CE)

Artabanus II had a long reign. He faced multiple rebellions, including a conflict with Vonones I, who tried to reclaim the crown with Roman backing. Artabanus II also dealt with issues in Armenia, fighting or negotiating with local rulers. At times, Roman emperors Tiberius and Caligula got involved, supporting whichever Armenian prince suited their aims.

Artabanus II managed to keep the Parthian state together despite these pressures. He used diplomacy to balance Roman interests, at one point even traveling west to meet Roman envoys halfway. Inside Parthia, he forged alliances with key noble families by giving them more estates or marrying into their lines. Though always tense, his rule showed that a capable king could still steer Parthia effectively.

---

9. Parthia at Its Strongest: Economic and Cultural Peak

Between the late 1st century BCE and the mid-1st century CE, Parthia was at its economic high point. The Silk Road trade was thriving, passing through major Parthian cities like **Hecatompylos**, **Ctesiphon**, and older centers like **Seleucia**. Merchant caravans arrived from China loaded with silk, lacquerware, and spices, while goods from the Roman Empire—wine, glass, precious metals—moved east. Parthian middlemen profited from taxes, protection fees, and the sale of local products like carpets, dates, gems, and high-quality horses.

Ctesiphon itself became a bustling metropolis, eventually overshadowing Seleucia across the river. Parthian kings and nobles built new palaces, mansions, and temples. Craftsmen mixed Greek, Iranian, and Mesopotamian techniques, producing unique art forms. Painted pottery, silverware with hunting scenes, and intricately carved rhytons (drinking vessels) all reflected the empire's blended culture.

In rural areas, landowners expanded irrigation, especially in Mesopotamia's fertile plains. This boosted agriculture, feeding the growing cities. Estates often had large barns for warhorses, essential to the Parthian cavalry tradition. Freedoms granted to local communities meant that villages kept some of their own traditions, as long as taxes were paid and local aristocrats obeyed the king's commands.

---

10. Interaction with Rome: Peace and Occasional War

Parthia's peak also coincided with the rise of the Roman Empire under Augustus and his successors. Both sides realized that constant war would be costly, and neither could fully conquer the other's main heartland. Thus, a pattern emerged: periods of relative peace, punctuated by local conflicts in places like Armenia or small-scale border skirmishes.

When diplomatic relations were smooth, Roman merchants traveled safely through Parthian lands to reach the Far East, and Parthian ambassadors visited Rome to negotiate trade deals. Some members of Parthian royal or noble families even stayed in Rome as "guests" (effectively hostages) to ensure good behavior back home. Roman historians like Tacitus and Josephus mention these visits, noting the exotic clothing and customs of the Parthians in the streets of Rome.

Still, each side was quick to exploit any sign of weakness. If the Roman emperor was busy with internal troubles, Parthia might push its advantage in Armenia. If a Parthian king faced a succession crisis, Rome might back a rival. This careful dance of power defined their relationship throughout the 1st century CE, with neither side able to dominate the other fully.

11. Religious and Philosophical Influences

The height of Parthian power also saw religious and philosophical ideas crossing borders. From the west came Greek schools of thought like Stoicism and Epicureanism, occasionally appealing to wealthy elites in Parthian cities. From the east, possibly from India and Central Asia, came various spiritual practices, including some early Buddhist influences, though these did not gain a wide following in Parthia.

Meanwhile, older Iranian traditions persisted. Some temples honored **Mithra**, a god associated with the sun, justice, and covenants. Mithraic symbols were sometimes carved on rock reliefs or minted on coins to show the king's favor. Babylonian astrology also remained popular, mixing Greek star lore with Mesopotamian beliefs. The result was a colorful religious environment where different faiths coexisted, especially in big trade hubs.

The Parthian kings did not impose a state religion. Instead, they let each region follow its own customs, as long as it did not threaten the king's authority. This approach mirrored earlier Achaemenid traditions of tolerance, although it was more a matter of practicality than a formal policy.

12. Royal Women and Courtly Influence

While Parthian society placed great emphasis on male warriors and nobles, royal women also held power behind the scenes. Queens and royal concubines could shape politics by supporting one prince over another for the throne. They forged alliances with noble houses, sometimes from their own families, and used their positions to grant favors or settle disputes.

Musa, for example, was an Italian slave girl given to Phraates IV by Augustus. She became a favored wife and bore Phraates a son. Over time, Musa gained enough influence to persuade Phraates IV to send his older sons to Rome. This cleared the path for Musa's son to become heir. Eventually, Musa and her son murdered Phraates IV and briefly ruled together as co-monarchs. Although their rule did not last long, it highlights how royal women could orchestrate dramatic shifts in the balance of power.

At the local level, noblewomen could also manage estates and represent their families in court events. Though overshadowed by men in official roles, their wealth and family ties often granted them a hidden influence that shaped the empire's history in subtle ways.

13. Seeds of Future Troubles

Despite its prosperity, Parthia at its peak contained weaknesses that would lead to problems in later decades. Here are a few:

1. **Decentralized Structure**: Giving extensive power to noble families worked well when a capable king held the throne, but it risked instability when that king was weak, old, or absent.
2. **Conflict Over Succession**: Without a fixed rule for choosing the next king, repeated crises arose. Brothers, uncles, and cousins all claimed the right to succeed. Nobles could back one claimant, Rome might back another, and yet another might gather support in the eastern provinces.
3. **Pressure from Nomads**: On the empire's northeastern frontiers, nomadic groups or semi-nomadic tribes could move in if local satraps were weak or if the king could not dispatch troops quickly.
4. **Border with Rome**: Although Parthia often defended itself successfully, the presence of a strong Roman Empire to the west meant constant vigilance. A single defeat or internal conflict could tempt Rome to invade deeper into Mesopotamia.

In the short term, strong rulers like Phraates IV or Artabanus II could manage these pressures. But as time passed, internal struggles and external wars would wear down Parthian resilience. Eventually, new powers—especially the **Sasanians**—would take advantage of these cracks in Parthia's foundation.

CHAPTER 12

CONFLICTS WITH ROME AND THE DECLINE OF PARTHIA

Introduction

In the previous chapter, we examined how the Parthian Empire reached its height, managing vast territories with the help of powerful noble families. They forged a dynamic relationship with Rome—sometimes waging war, sometimes keeping the peace—while trade along the Silk Road enriched cities and merchants. Despite these strengths, Parthian rule was never fully stable. Internal rivalries, a loose confederation of noble houses, and repeated succession crises left the empire open to foreign pressure.

Now, we turn to the last stages of the Parthian Empire. Over the 1st and 2nd centuries CE, Roman Emperors like Trajan, Hadrian, and Marcus Aurelius tested Parthian power, launching major campaigns into Mesopotamia. Parthian kings, in turn, sought to influence Rome's eastern provinces and keep Armenia under their sway. But repeated internal strife made it hard for Parthia to present a united front. By the 3rd century CE, a new threat emerged from inside Iran itself: the **Sasanian** movement, led by ambitious local rulers who claimed to restore the old Persian (Achaemenid) traditions. Under leaders like **Ardashir I**, the Sasanians challenged and finally toppled the Parthian dynasty.

In this chapter, we will follow the key conflicts between Rome and Parthia, focusing on major invasions and how each side responded. We will see how frequent civil wars in the Parthian court weakened the empire's defenses, and how local dissatisfaction fueled support for the new Sasanian cause. We will conclude with the fall of the Arsacid line, signaling the end of Parthian rule and the start of a new chapter in Persia's story.

1. Rome Looks East: The 1st Century CE

During the early 1st century CE, relations between Rome and Parthia often revolved around Armenia. As we learned, Armenia was a buffer zone with its own royal family, sometimes linked to the Parthians. Roman Emperors like Tiberius and Claudius tried to place friendly rulers on the Armenian throne, while Parthian kings did the same. This tug-of-war created constant friction. However, full-scale wars remained rare until **Nero** became emperor (54–68 CE).

Nero and Armenia

In the late 50s CE, the Parthian king **Vologases I** supported his brother Tiridates as king of Armenia, challenging Rome's candidate. Roman general Corbulo marched in and captured the Armenian capital, forcing Tiridates to leave. Vologases I, distracted by nomad invasions in the east, decided not to fight Rome head-on. Eventually, a compromise was reached: Tiridates visited Rome, recognized Nero as the supreme overlord, and then went back to Armenia as the recognized king. This arrangement saved face for both sides—Rome kept nominal authority, while Armenia functioned as a Parthian ally.

Vologases I's approach shows the flexibility of Parthian diplomacy. Instead of risking a massive war they might lose, the Parthians were willing to sign deals that maintained influence under a Roman umbrella. Still, the arrangement was fragile, depending on continuing goodwill or mutual weakness.

---

2. The Rise of the Roman Emperors Trajan and Hadrian

In 98 CE, **Trajan** became the Roman Emperor. He was an ambitious military leader who wanted to expand Rome's frontiers, especially in the wealthy East. Trajan believed that conquering Mesopotamia would give Rome control over important trade routes. The Parthians at the time were dealing with internal issues once again, including disputes over who should be king. This gave Trajan an opening.

Trajan's Invasion (113–117 CE)

Around 113 CE, Trajan used a dispute over the Armenian throne as a pretext for war. Roman legions advanced into Armenia, defeated local forces, and declared it a Roman province. They then pushed into northern Mesopotamia, capturing cities like Nisibis and Edessa, annexing these areas into new provinces. Finally, Trajan marched down the Euphrates, took the great city of **Ctesiphon** (the Parthian capital area), and even reached the shores of the Persian Gulf.

For a moment, it seemed Rome might have fully conquered Parthia. However, holding these lands proved harder than taking them. Local Parthian nobles rose in revolt behind Roman lines, capturing or killing Roman garrisons. The climate was tough for Roman troops, and supply lines were overstretched. In 117 CE, Trajan died during his return journey, leaving his conquests in disarray.

Hadrian's Withdrawal

Trajan's successor, **Hadrian** (117–138 CE), saw that these new territories were too costly to defend. He decided to withdraw from most of Mesopotamia and Armenia, returning them to local rulers or Parthian influence. Hadrian preferred a stable frontier over indefinite wars far from Rome's core. This gave the Parthians breathing room to regroup and reassert control in Mesopotamia. They had lost face by letting Trajan take their capital, but Rome's retreat showed that permanent occupation would be difficult for even the mightiest empire.

3. Parthian Internal Struggles in the 2nd Century CE

Even though Parthia survived Trajan's invasion, the empire was not unified. Royal family quarrels and noble rebellions kept springing up. Different factions supported different princes. One king, **Vologases III**, ruled at the same time as another, **Osroes I**, each claiming legitimacy in different parts of the empire. Some local satraps might recognize one, while others recognized the other. This chaos made it easier for Rome to intervene whenever it wanted an advantage.

Nobles and the Power Vacuum

Because the Parthian monarchy was not strongly centralized, local nobles grew bolder. In some regions, these nobles acted almost like independent kings, minting their own coins and making treaties with neighboring peoples. The monarchy tried to curb these tendencies by granting or revoking titles, but the absence of a regular system for royal succession meant that every time a king died, or appeared weak, multiple claimants stepped forward.

This environment also hurt the empire economically. While trade continued along the Silk Road, some merchants avoided traveling through areas with constant civil strife. Internal wars damaged farmland, caravans, and infrastructure like roads or bridges. Over time, these disruptions chipped away at the wealth that had once made Parthia strong.

---

4. The Reign of Vologases IV and Continued Roman-Parthian Wars

By around 147 CE, **Vologases IV** became the dominant ruler of Parthia, managing to unify much of the empire under his name. He tried to consolidate power, handle the ever-problematic question of Armenia, and maintain Parthian prestige. But Roman Emperors like **Lucius Verus** (co-emperor with Marcus Aurelius) saw an opportunity.

Lucius Verus's Campaign (162–166 CE)

When Vologases IV placed his own candidate on the Armenian throne, Rome again declared war. The Roman co-emperor Lucius Verus led an army into Mesopotamia in 162 CE, capturing major cities like **Seleucia** and **Ctesiphon** once more. The Romans reportedly sacked the Parthian palace, taking loot and burning property. However, an outbreak of plague among the Roman troops forced them to retreat, limiting their gains.

Still, this invasion underlined Parthia's vulnerability whenever it lacked firm leadership or internal unity. Each time Rome advanced, the Parthians were forced into defensive action, often losing their capital or key trade routes. Even if Rome did not stay permanently, the repeated invasions caused massive disruptions for the local population.

Cultural Consequences of War

These wars also had a cultural impact. Each occupation or sack of cities like Ctesiphon destroyed libraries, temples, or palatial art. Skilled artisans fled or were taken captive to Roman lands. This damage chipped away at the Parthian cultural centers that had flourished earlier. Local resentment grew against the royal court for failing to protect them, while some nobles switched allegiances to Rome or tried to form their own smaller states.

---

5. The Rise of Vologases V and Septimius Severus

Vologases V came to the throne around 191 CE. By that time, Rome was ruled by **Septimius Severus** (193–211 CE), a tough soldier-emperor who wanted to boost his prestige by campaigning in the East.

Severus's Campaign

Between 195 and 198 CE, Septimius Severus launched invasions into Parthian territory. He used disagreements over the Armenian throne as a justification, similar to previous Roman emperors. Severus led a strong Roman army that again captured **Seleucia** and **Ctesiphon**, plundering the region. Although the Parthians resisted with cavalry raids, they could not prevent the Romans from briefly occupying large parts of Mesopotamia.

Severus eventually pulled back, content with loot and the propaganda victory of claiming to have defeated Parthia. He also established a Roman province called **Mesopotamia** in the northern section, around Nisibis and Singara, further shrinking Parthian control in the area. This blow showed how far the Parthian Empire had declined from its peak, when it had successfully handled Roman threats.

Internal Weakness Grows

Repeated defeats at the hands of Rome discredited the Arsacid ruling family in the eyes of many Parthian nobles. The monarchy seemed unable to protect Mesopotamia or to push Rome back across the Euphrates for good. Tax burdens rose to pay for defense, upsetting both nobles (who had to raise troops) and peasants (who faced heavier levies on crops).

Meanwhile, local powers in eastern Iran also sensed the central government's growing weakness. Some areas in the southeast recognized only nominal Parthian authority, and small local dynasties took charge of day-to-day governance. Even the vital Silk Road trade began to shift routes away from war-torn regions, reducing the revenue that once flowed into the royal coffers.

6. The Emergence of the House of Sāsān in Fars

While the Parthian kings struggled against Rome, a local Persian family in the region of **Fars** (the ancient homeland of the Achaemenids) was quietly expanding its power. This family, linked to a man named **Sāsān**, rose to prominence under his descendant, **Papak** (or Babak), who governed a small district. They claimed lineage from the ancient gods or heroes revered in older Iranian religion, possibly seeking to connect themselves to the memory of the Achaemenids, who once ruled a grand empire from the same region.

Ardashir I Takes Center Stage

The true force behind the new movement was **Ardashir I**, the son or stepson of Papak. Ardashir I built alliances with neighboring local rulers, then moved to conquer more territories in southwestern Iran. He presented himself as a champion of old Persian traditions, criticizing the Parthians for letting foreigners (like the Romans) repeatedly invade and for failing to uphold a strong Iranian kingship.

By around 220 CE, Ardashir I was powerful enough to challenge the Parthian monarchy directly. King **Artabanus IV** (a later Arsacid) recognized the threat and tried to stop Ardashir's expansion. In 224 CE, the two sides met in a decisive battle near Hormizdegan (in southwestern Iran). Ardashir's forces prevailed, and Artabanus IV was killed. This victory ended the Arsacid line's long reign over Iran, ushering in the **Sasanian** era.

---

7. Why Did the Parthians Fall?

The fall of the Parthian Empire was not the result of a single event but rather a slow erosion of power over many decades. Some key reasons include:

1. **Decentralized System**: The reliance on a loose network of nobles and local dynasties worked well under strong kings but collapsed when weaker or short-lived kings allowed powerful families to act independently.
2. **Succession Crises**: Without a stable method for choosing the next king, almost every royal death or major setback led to multiple claimants. Civil wars drained resources and caused chaos.
3. **Roman Pressure**: Although Rome did not conquer all of Parthia, repeated invasions shattered the empire's prestige and caused material damage. The capital region was sacked multiple times, undermining the royal court.
4. **Local Revolts in the East**: Regions like Fars, where the future Sasanians arose, grew tired of Parthian mismanagement and war losses. Ambitious local leaders capitalized on the monarchy's vulnerability.
5. **Loss of Trade**: Warfare and instability made trade routes less profitable. Noble families also took a bigger share of taxes for their own armies, leaving the central government weaker financially.

By the time Ardashir I confronted the last Parthian king, many nobles and local rulers in Iran saw the Sasanians as a welcome change—perhaps a chance to restore a more unified and proudly "Persian" monarchy, recalling the glories of Cyrus the Great and Darius I.

8. The Final Years and Legacy of the Arsacid Dynasty

Even after Artabanus IV's death, some members of the Arsacid family tried to hang on in remote parts of the empire. However, Ardashir I and his son **Shapur I** methodically defeated any remaining Arsacid loyalists. By the early 3rd century CE, the Sasanian dynasty was firmly in control of Iran, Mesopotamia, and other key regions once held by the Parthians.

The Arsacid line did not vanish completely: one branch continued to rule in Armenia for centuries, maintaining an Armenian Arsacid dynasty. In other regions, certain noble houses traced their ancestry back to the Parthians, blending into the new Sasanian order. Despite losing power, the Parthians left a lasting mark on the region's culture, military traditions, and sense of Iranian identity.

Over nearly five centuries, the Parthians had acted as a bridge between the Hellenistic world of Alexander's successors and the later medieval Islamic powers that would rise in the same region. Their acceptance of local diversity, skillful cavalry warfare, and flexible approach to governance offered a distinct model of empire. Their downfall showed that no empire, however strong, could survive without robust political structures, stable successions, and the ability to defend against repeated external invasions.

9. Parthian Cultural Contributions

Even as the Sasanian Empire took shape, people continued to remember the cultural achievements of the Parthians. Some of these contributions include:

- **Art and Architecture**: Parthian-era styles influenced Sasanian art, particularly in the way figures were depicted in relief sculptures and in certain architectural forms like the iwan.
- **Military Tactics**: The famous Parthian cavalry traditions did not disappear. The Sasanians continued to field heavy armored cavalry (clibanarii or cataphracts) and used some of the same strategies of mobility and archery.
- **Religious Pluralism**: The Parthians had allowed multiple faiths to thrive. Although the Sasanians promoted a more official form of Zoroastrianism, the idea of diverse religious communities under a single crown remained an ongoing reality in the region.
- **Political Memory**: Some Iranians looked back on the Parthians as defenders against Rome. Poems, legends, and local tales recounted heroic battles. Others, especially in the Sasanian court, criticized the Parthians as decentralized and weak. Both views shaped later Persian historical writing.

---

10. Transition to the Sasanian Era

When Ardashir I crowned himself "Shahanshah" (King of Kings) of the new Sasanian Empire, he declared a return to the glories of ancient Persia. He aligned himself with a more structured form of Zoroastrianism, rebuilt major cities, and enacted reforms that gave the central government tighter control. Many Parthian nobles either joined the Sasanian system or lost their lands and titles.

In the next chapters, we will see how the Sasanian Empire grew into one of the most formidable powers of the late ancient world, matching and sometimes surpassing the accomplishments of earlier dynasties. However, the long centuries of Parthian rule remained a key part of Iran's historical tapestry. From the famed Parthian shot to their diplomatic balancing act with Rome, the Arsacid dynasty left a distinct stamp on the region's political and cultural identity.

Conclusion of Chapter 12

In this chapter, we traced Parthia's final centuries as it faced constant Roman pressure, internal divisions, and the eventual rise of the Sasanian dynasty. While strong kings like Vologases IV and Vologases V tried to hold the empire together, repeated invasions and sacking of major cities drained Parthia's resources and prestige. The lack of a stable succession process led to civil wars, opening the door for local powers like the House of Sāsān in Fars to challenge the Arsacid line.

Finally, in 224 CE, Ardashir I defeated Artabanus IV, ending the Parthian era. Though the Arsacids lost their throne, their cultural and military heritage influenced the new Sasanian Empire and shaped the broader history of the region. Parthia's story is one of remarkable endurance, bridging the Hellenistic period and the rise of medieval Persia. It shows that even a loosely organized empire can stand against mighty foes if it masters cavalry warfare, forms pragmatic alliances, and embraces diversity—yet it also reveals the dangers of weak succession and internal strife.

CHAPTER 13

THE FALL OF THE PARTHIAN EMPIRE

Introduction

In the previous chapter, we explored how the Parthian Empire dealt with rising pressures from Rome and from internal power struggles. We saw how repeated invasions by ambitious Roman emperors—like Trajan and Septimius Severus—along with constant succession crises, began to weaken the once-formidable Arsacid Dynasty.

Now, in Chapter 13, we will focus on the **final decades** of the Parthian Empire and examine how it truly fell. Although we touched on the theme of decline before, here we step more deeply into the **complex web** of civil conflicts, shifting noble alliances, and local revolts that doomed the Arsacid rulers. We will look at how a new power center rose in the region of Fars (Persis), led first by local lords and then by the ambitious leader **Ardashir I**. In a dramatic confrontation on the battlefield, Ardashir I defeated the last major Parthian king, **Artabanus IV**, ending centuries of Arsacid rule.

By the close of this chapter, we will see how the Parthian Empire, despite a proud legacy of cavalry warfare and regional diplomacy, collapsed under the weight of internal divisions and the rise of a more unified, determined power. This sets the stage for the next era of Persian history: the rule of the **Sasanian** kings, who would build a new empire on the ashes of the old.

1. A Fragile Empire at Its Limits

Parthian power reached its peak in the 1st century BCE and the early 1st century CE, largely under kings like Orodes II, Phraates IV, and Vologases IV. But over time, the empire's loose structure began to show signs of **deep internal weakness**. Some of these issues had been present for centuries, but they grew more severe as the empire faced repeated crises.

Decentralized Governance

The Parthian model depended on a confederation of powerful noble families. The Arsacid king acted as a "first among equals" in many respects, and local rulers (often called satraps or regional lords) enjoyed a high degree of autonomy. While this system had advantages—it could quickly gather troops from noble estates—it also meant that the empire's stability heavily relied on the loyalty of these nobles.

If a Parthian king was strong, he might keep the nobles united. But a weak or unpopular monarch often found that major families sought to install a different ruler from the extended Arsacid line, sometimes with foreign help. No well-defined law of succession existed, so a king's death or defeat could lead to multiple claimants battling for power.

Frequent Succession Disputes

With no fixed rule for inheritance, the throne of Parthia passed from father to son—or from uncle to nephew, brother to brother—based on who could gain enough noble support. This led to **constant internal quarrels**. One example is the rivalry between Phraates IV and his relatives, which forced the king to take extreme measures like executing potential rivals or sending them to Rome as "guests" (effectively hostages).

Such violence scared other nobles, who felt the king's paranoia could turn on them. In return, some nobles turned to foreign powers, including Rome, for support. This cycle of mistrust and betrayal prevented the empire from unifying around long-term projects like improving roads, reforming taxes, or strengthening frontiers.

Roman Pressure and Prestige Loss

Rome repeatedly invaded Parthian lands, sacking key cities like Ctesiphon. While Rome rarely held these conquests for very long, such invasions damaged the Parthian reputation for protecting local populations. The monarchy claimed to be the guardian of Iran and Mesopotamia, but if the Romans could march in and seize the capital every few decades, people lost confidence in the Arsacid house.

The cost of defending against Rome was enormous. Kings had to raise taxes to maintain armies, causing unrest among nobles and peasants alike. War-torn provinces generated less revenue. Over time, these disruptions weakened the empire's economic base, fueling even more resentment and rebellion.

Local Revolts and Eastern Discontent
While Rome threatened from the west, tribes and small dynasties in the east, including nomadic groups near the Oxus River or local rulers in Sistan and Fars, also challenged central authority. Some of these groups had supported the Arsacids originally but found Parthian governance inadequate. They might have paid tribute reluctantly, always searching for a chance to break free.

By the 2nd century CE, a new class of local leaders gained prominence in Fars. They celebrated ancient Persian traditions and saw the Parthians as foreign usurpers who had never fully embraced the old Achaemenid ideals. This discontent created fertile ground for a bold, charismatic leader to rally supporters and claim the right to rule Iran in a more unified, national sense.

---

2. The Rise of the House of Sāsān in Fars

Among the various local powers on the Iranian Plateau, one small realm in **Fars (also known as Persis)** began to stand out. This was the homeland of the ancient Achaemenid kings Cyrus the Great and Darius I. Even centuries later, many families in Fars preserved a sense of connection to that glorious past. They honored the memory of Persepolis, still visible in ruins. They told stories of the old Persian kings who had once ruled a vast empire.

Sāsān and Papak

A man named **Sāsān** (sometimes spelled Sassan) headed a local religious or noble lineage. He may have served as a guardian of a fire temple in the region, giving him spiritual authority among the population. Through alliances or marriage, Sāsān's family rose to become important in Fars.

Papak (or Babak), possibly Sāsān's son or son-in-law, inherited or expanded Sāsān's authority. Papak carved out a bigger domain, taking smaller neighboring districts under his control. He built a network of loyalty by rewarding local lords and presenting himself as a restorer of true Iranian values—a theme that resonated in a time when the Parthian kings were losing face against Rome.

Ardashir I's Ambitions

The real driving force behind the House of Sāsān was **Ardashir I**, Papak's son (or step-son). From a young age, Ardashir showed talent in military leadership and statecraft. He led successful raids against local rivals and strengthened the fortifications of key towns in Fars. At first, the Parthian monarchy barely noticed him, being too busy with bigger problems in Mesopotamia.

As Ardashir's power grew, he attracted warriors and nobles who were dissatisfied with the Parthian system. Some sought to escape heavy taxes; others hoped to join a rising star who might replace a shaky regime. By about 220 CE, Ardashir had become the dominant figure in Fars and was looking beyond his home province.

A Call to Revive "Pure Persian" Rule

A key part of Ardashir's appeal was the notion that he was reviving the old Persian kingship once held by Cyrus and Darius. He tapped into the shared memory of the Achaemenids as a time when Iran had led a mighty empire with strong cultural identity. Stories spread that Ardashir had divine favor or that he was destined to overthrow the weak, foreign-influenced Parthians.

This "national" or cultural rhetoric, though not exactly the same as modern ideas of nationalism, still fired people's imaginations. Many Iranian nobles disliked how the Parthians allowed Greek and Mesopotamian elements to dominate court life or how they had lost city after city to Rome. Ardashir promised a fresh start, with firmer leadership and a spiritual dimension linked to Iranian religious traditions (which would later be associated with a more formal Zoroastrian clergy).

---

3. Artabanus IV and the Last Parthian Stand

By the early 3rd century CE, the Arsacid throne was held (in most regions) by **Artabanus IV**. He faced the typical swirl of challenges—local revolts, Roman interference, and friction with other Arsacid claimants. But now, Ardashir's rise in Fars demanded his full attention. A new Persian power threatened the monarchy from within.

Initial Skirmishes
At first, Artabanus IV might have dismissed Ardashir as just another rebellious satrap. However, as word came that Ardashir was conquering neighboring provinces and forging alliances, the king realized the danger. Artabanus tried to rally the major Parthian noble houses to crush the revolt before it spread.

The two sides engaged in **initial battles** in central and southern Iran. Ardashir's forces, well-trained in the rugged terrain of Fars, proved more disciplined than expected. They employed cavalry tactics reminiscent of Parthian warfare itself—swift horse archers and heavily armored riders—but with a new sense of unity under Ardashir's command. Parthian generals were surprised to find themselves outmaneuvered by someone using adapted versions of their own strategies.

Noble Defections
Some Parthian nobles, tired of the endless civil wars and Roman invasions, began to desert Artabanus IV's cause. They saw Ardashir as a potential savior who could provide a more centralized and stable rule. If the monarchy had lost the support of enough key lords, it was only a matter of time before the old system collapsed.

Moreover, Ardashir's promises of renewed wealth and strong leadership enticed lesser nobles who had felt overlooked under the Parthians. He offered them positions in his new administration, guaranteeing them lands and titles in exchange for loyalty. Artabanus IV scrambled to keep his coalition intact, but internal distrust ran high.

The Showdown at Hormizdegan (224 CE)
Realizing the threat could no longer be contained with minor skirmishes, Artabanus IV led a major Parthian army to confront Ardashir's forces. The decisive battle took place at **Hormizdegan**, likely near modern-day Shushtar or in southwestern Iran.

Accounts differ on the details, but most agree that Ardashir's army displayed superior organization and morale. His cavalry hammered the Parthian lines, and many of Artabanus's soldiers either fled or switched sides. In the end, Artabanus IV was killed in the fighting, sealing the fate of the Arsacid Dynasty. Having won a spectacular victory, Ardashir marched north to claim the old Parthian capitals, proclaiming himself **Shahanshah** (King of Kings).

4. The Final Collapse of the Arsacid Line

After Hormizdegan, the Parthian Empire effectively ceased to exist as a unified state. Some Arsacid princes may have attempted to keep control of remote areas, but Ardashir rapidly moved to **consolidate his power**.

Mopping-Up Operations
Ardashir dispatched loyal generals to Mesopotamia, Media, and other key provinces. They negotiated or fought with local Parthian governors, demanding their submission. Many complied, seeing that Artabanus IV was gone and that continuing to resist would only invite harsh punishment. Others tried to hold out but soon found themselves isolated.

Arsacid Legacy in Armenia
While the Arsacids lost Iran, one branch of the family continued to rule in Armenia for centuries. This Armenian Arsacid line maintained partial independence, though it was often caught between the new Sasanian Empire and Rome. The fact that an Arsacid dynasty

survived in Armenia is a reminder that the Parthian house did not vanish overnight. However, their power outside Armenia was finished.

Ardashir's Coronation and New Order

By 226 CE, Ardashir was formally crowned in a grand ceremony. He took on titles emphasizing his place as the successor to the Achaemenids, claiming divine support and championing a **renewed Iranian identity**. Zoroastrian priests played a significant role in these rituals, symbolizing a tighter link between religion and the throne than had existed under the Parthians. This signaled the dawn of the **Sasanian Empire**, which would dominate Iran and beyond for the next four centuries.

5. Reasons for the Parthian Fall: Deeper Insights

Looking back, why did Parthia—so strong it had humbled Rome on multiple occasions—ultimately fall to an internal challenger?

Loss of Military Confidence

The Parthians had prided themselves on their cavalry tactics, but they faced repeated defeats or stalemates against Rome. Each time the Romans sacked Ctesiphon, local populations questioned whether the king could defend them. Meanwhile, Ardashir modernized cavalry forces and employed strategies that combined the best of Parthian, local Iranian, and even Roman methods (such as better organization and siege techniques).

Failure to Reform

Even though the Parthian system worked for a long time, it **never evolved** into a more cohesive state. Other empires in the region (like

Rome) had developed bureaucracies, codified laws, and clearer processes for handling successions. Parthia, however, stuck with a tradition-bound approach that left everything dependent on personal relationships and family ties. This approach finally collapsed under the strain of near-constant warfare.

Emergence of a Charismatic Rival
Ardashir I's success was not just about the system's weaknesses; it was also about **his own strengths**. He possessed vision, ruthlessness, and the ability to inspire loyalty. He fashioned a rallying cry based on reviving the glory of ancient Persia, which resonated deeply with the Iranian nobility and commoners alike, especially after so many humiliations under the later Parthian kings.

Shift in Economic Power
As the Parthians struggled with internal wars, certain regions—especially southwestern Iran—grew wealthier and more independent. Trade routes could bypass war-torn areas, and local rulers used that income to build private armies. By the time Artabanus IV recognized the threat from Fars, it was too late: Ardashir had already built a powerful economic base and a loyal following of soldiers.

---

6. The Aftermath for Parthian Nobles and Cities

The end of Arsacid rule did not mean a complete cultural reset. Many Parthian aristocrats **transitioned** into Sasanian service if they pledged loyalty to Ardashir. Others fled to outlying regions or into Roman territory, hoping to avoid retribution.

- **Cities like Ctesiphon** changed hands without being destroyed. Ardashir recognized the strategic and commercial value of these urban centers and kept them as part of his new empire.

- **Some Parthian traditions** in art, clothing, and cavalry continued under the Sasanians, though now framed within a more centralized and ideologically driven monarchy.
- **The memory of Parthian heroes** still lived on in local stories and in some border zones, where old loyalties died hard. But the crown had unmistakably shifted to a new dynasty, one determined to reshape Iran's future.

7. Legacy of the Parthian Empire

While the Arsacid line ended in Iran, the Parthian legacy remained:

1. **Military Tactics**: The famous "Parthian shot" and heavy cavalry (cataphracts) influenced the Sasanian army, and even beyond, affecting Roman and Byzantine military strategies for centuries.
2. **Cultural Fusion**: The Parthians had long blended Iranian, Hellenistic, and Mesopotamian elements. This fusion did not vanish; it flowed into the Sasanian era and shaped the region's diverse artistic heritage.

3. **Diplomacy with Rome**: Parthia pioneered a pattern of dealing with Rome that the Sasanians would inherit—alternating between war and negotiation, with Armenia often at the center.
4. **Noble Autonomy**: The Parthian system of powerful regional lords influenced how the Sasanians managed their nobility. Although the Sasanians aimed to centralize power more tightly, they still had to reckon with influential aristocrats.

In many ways, the fall of Parthia was also the birth of a new Persian empire that took the lessons of the past—both the achievements and failures—and forged a more unified state. As we move forward, we will see how the Sasanian kings molded these legacies into a dynasty that rivaled Rome and Byzantium for centuries, leaving a profound impact on Middle Eastern history.

CHAPTER 14

THE BEGINNING OF THE SASANIAN EMPIRE

Introduction

We concluded Chapter 13 with the fall of the Parthian Empire under the final Arsacid king, Artabanus IV, defeated by **Ardashir I** at the Battle of Hormizdegan in 224 CE. Ardashir's triumph signaled the start of a new era in Persian history—the **Sasanian Empire**. In this chapter, we will explore how Ardashir I established his rule, overcame remaining pockets of Arsacid resistance, and shaped a new royal identity grounded in references to ancient Achaemenid tradition and strengthened by religious ties to Zoroastrianism.

As we begin, keep in mind that the Sasanian transformation did not happen overnight. While Ardashir quickly seized the Parthian heartlands, building a stable empire required years of conquest, negotiation, and careful management of local elites. We will see how Ardashir worked to unify the Iranian Plateau under a single crown, set up administrative reforms, and develop a more centralized approach to governance than the Parthians had. Finally, we will look at how the Sasanian monarchy fashioned a new image for Persian kings—one that combined the memory of ancient Persia with fresh symbols of royal and divine authority.

1. Ardashir I's Early Moves: Consolidating Power

After his victory over Artabanus IV, Ardashir I wasted no time in **securing his hold** on the lands once claimed by the Parthians.

Occupation of Major Cities

Ardashir marched north from the southwestern battlefields, entering key cities in Mesopotamia and Media (northwestern Iran). Wherever he arrived, he demanded that local governors acknowledge him as **Shahanshah** ("King of Kings"). In regions that surrendered peacefully, Ardashir generally spared the local elites, allowing them to keep some power if they pledged loyalty and paid tribute. In areas that resisted, he used force to remove any Parthian loyalists still clinging to authority.

Dealing with Residual Arsacid Princes

Some members of the Arsacid family tried to regroup, hoping to spark a counter-revolt. Ardashir sent trusted generals to hunt down these potential rivals, offering clemency to those who submitted but punishing stubborn holdouts. Within a year or two, most serious Arsacid challengers had either fled (some to Armenia) or been subdued.

Diplomacy with the Nobility

A vital step in building a new empire was **negotiating with local noble families**. Ardashir needed their support to collect taxes, raise armies, and maintain law and order. Although he aimed for more centralized control than the Parthians had, he recognized that total disregard for the nobility could spark widespread rebellion. Hence, he struck bargains: those nobles who recognized his sovereignty could keep their estates and titles, provided they served the new order.

Through these maneuvers, Ardashir stabilized the core of his new empire, from Fars in the south to Media in the northwest and Mesopotamia in the west. By about 226–227 CE, he was ready to proclaim a fresh imperial identity that broke decisively with the Parthian past.

2. Crafting the Sasanian Ideology

Ardashir I understood that conquering lands was one thing—**legitimizing** his rule on a grand scale was another. He set out to create an empire-wide narrative that portrayed him as the rightful heir to ancient Persian kings, favored by the highest divine powers.

Connection to the Achaemenids

Even though the Achaemenid dynasty had ended centuries earlier under Alexander the Great, their memory still loomed large in Persian culture. Ardashir's propagandists spread stories linking his ancestry to the old Persian heroes. They claimed he was reviving the line of Cyrus and Darius. In official rock reliefs, Ardashir had himself depicted receiving the "ring of kingship" from Ahura Mazda—an image reminiscent of how Darius I had once been portrayed in royal inscriptions.

Role of Zoroastrianism

During Parthian times, Zoroastrian practices existed but were not strongly centralized. Ardashir wanted a closer tie between the throne and the faith. **Zoroastrian priests** who backed him gained status as important state advisors. Ardashir encouraged the collection and systematization of Zoroastrian texts, aiming to define a "true" form of worship that supported the monarchy's legitimacy. This set in motion a gradual process that would solidify Zoroastrianism as the Sasanian "state religion" in the decades to come.

Royal Imagery and Titles

Ardashir adopted grand titles like "Shahanshah of Iran" and sometimes even added "non-Iran"—suggesting ambitions to rule beyond the traditional Iranian Plateau. Some inscriptions used phrases that hearkened back to the glory of the old Persian Empire.

Court ceremonies were made more elaborate, with the king wearing a distinctive crown or diadem and royal robes that distinguished him from any noble.

In doing so, Ardashir built a clear hierarchy: **the king** (selected by divine grace) at the top, **nobles and priests** who supported him below, and **commoners** who benefited from stable government. He hoped this structure would prevent the fractious noble autonomy that had plagued the Parthians.

---

3. Early Sasanian Administration: More Centralization

One of the main criticisms of the Parthian system was its patchwork governance. Ardashir I sought to address this by creating or expanding administrative offices that answered directly to the crown.

Satraps vs. Royal Appointees

Like the Achaemenids and Parthians, the Sasanians still used the term "satrap" (or a similar title) for provincial governors. However, Ardashir's key difference lay in **closer supervision**. He placed loyal family members or tested generals as governors over crucial provinces. Where possible, he reduced the power of local hereditary dynasties, requiring them to accept a royal representative or marry into his own family.

Taxes and Revenue

A well-organized empire needed consistent tax revenue. Ardashir introduced reforms to standardize tax rates on agricultural land, trade caravans, and urban crafts. He assigned royal inspectors to ensure local governors did not cheat the treasury or exploit the people too severely. This approach allowed the central government to collect more resources to fund the army, build infrastructure, and reward loyal supporters.

Record-Keeping and Aramaic Influence

Parthian rulers had relied partly on Aramaic as an administrative language. The Sasanians continued to use Aramaic scripts in some areas, but they also promoted **Middle Persian (also called Pahlavi)** for official inscriptions and documents. Over time, Middle Persian replaced Greek or Parthian scripts in many administrative tasks. This language shift was part of Ardashir's broader push to create a more distinctly "Persian" imperial identity.

These administrative changes did not happen without resistance. Some local rulers bristled at a stronger central hand. But Ardashir's success on the battlefield gave him the clout to push these measures forward. If any region rebelled, the new monarchy swiftly dispatched armies to reassert control, signaling that the era of a loose confederation was gone.

---

4. Securing Borders and Handling the Parthian Aftermath

Although Ardashir I had defeated Artabanus IV, the new Sasanian Empire still faced challenges in securing its frontiers and stamping out any lingering Arsacid influences.

Conflict in Mesopotamia

While many Mesopotamian cities capitulated, some pockets of Parthian loyalists tried to hold out, hoping for Roman assistance. Ardashir responded by placing strong garrisons in strategic locations along the Euphrates. He built or repaired fortifications, preparing for the possibility that Rome might exploit any internal chaos to expand its holdings.

Armenia's Arsacid Dynasty

In **Armenia**, a separate branch of the Arsacid family continued to rule. They claimed partial independence, backed at times by Rome.

Ardashir did not immediately invade Armenia, possibly because he did not want to provoke a full-scale war with Rome just yet. Instead, he used diplomacy and threat, encouraging pro-Sasanian nobles in Armenia to undermine the local Arsacid king.

Eastern Provinces
On the eastern front, tribes and minor kingdoms near the Oxus River and in parts of modern Afghanistan had grown used to Parthian neglect. Ardashir dispatched envoys and small military contingents to remind them of the central government's authority. Some areas joined peacefully, while others had to be subdued. The main goal was to reestablish consistent taxation and to prevent these regions from becoming refuges for rebel forces.

By addressing each border zone quickly, Ardashir showed that he intended to rule a more cohesive empire than the Parthians had. He aimed to remove the perception that distant provinces could do as they pleased without interference from the royal court.

---

5. Religious and Cultural Shifts Under Ardashir I

While the Sasanian system built on many Parthian foundations, it also promoted new cultural and religious emphases to distinguish it from the past.

Strengthening Zoroastrian Institutions
Zoroastrian priests, known as **magi**, gained an elevated role in the Sasanian court. Ardashir encouraged them to compile and standardize religious texts, possibly laying the groundwork for the **Avesta**, the holy book of Zoroastrianism (though the final redaction would take place over a longer period). The king and the priests formed a symbiotic alliance:

- The monarchy gave the priests state support, including land grants and temple patronage.
- The priests endorsed the king's rule as sacred, portraying him as chosen by Ahura Mazda (the supreme god in Zoroastrian belief).

This close partnership gave Sasanian rulers a potent ideological tool to unify the empire. It also began to marginalize other religious communities, though such marginalization would intensify under later kings.

Revival of Persian Art Forms
Ardashir commissioned the construction of **fire temples**, palaces, and monumental rock reliefs across the empire. These reliefs often showed him or his generals defeating enemies or receiving divine sanction. They borrowed elements from older Iranian styles (like the Achaemenids) and from local traditions that had survived under the Parthians. Over time, Sasanian art developed a distinctive approach—frontal poses, richly patterned clothing, and grand ceremonial scenes.

Court Ceremonies and Etiquette
The Sasanian court introduced more **rituals** around the king's person. Attendants and courtiers had to follow strict forms of greeting and dress. The throne room displayed symbols of royal power, including a tall crown and a raised platform for the king, reinforcing the idea that he was far above the common people—and even above most nobles. This was a departure from the Parthian tradition, where the king often sat among the lords as a first among equals.

These cultural developments helped unify the realm under a single banner, creating a shared sense of Sasanian identity. Some local populations resented heavier control from the center, but many others welcomed the stability and the new grandeur after decades of Parthian infighting.

6. Relations with Rome in Ardashir's Time

The Roman Empire closely watched events in Persia. Having fought the Parthians repeatedly, Rome did not ignore the sudden rise of a new dynasty. Some Roman leaders assumed the Sasanians were just another short-lived faction. Others, more astute, realized that Ardashir's movement had genuine momentum.

Limited Skirmishes
Initial encounters between Sasanian and Roman forces were small-scale. Roman garrisons in northern Mesopotamia tested Sasanian defenses, while Ardashir's troops probed Roman fortresses. Neither side launched a major invasion yet—Ardashir needed to stabilize his empire, and Rome, under Emperor Severus Alexander (r. 222–235 CE), faced its own internal problems and threats along the Danube frontier.

Negotiations and Propaganda
Ardashir sent messengers to Rome, possibly offering peace on the condition that Rome recognize Sasanian authority over Mesopotamia and other former Parthian domains. Roman historians record that Ardashir also demanded all the lands once ruled by the Achaemenids, implying that Rome should relinquish certain eastern territories. This bold claim was more of a **propaganda** move, signaling that the Sasanians considered themselves the heirs of the entire ancient Persian Empire.

Rome rejected these demands, but for the moment, it did not escalate into a full-blown conflict. Both powers were wary of committing to a huge war they might not win. However, this cautious calm would not last forever; later Sasanian kings, like Ardashir's son **Shapur I**, would test Rome's strength more aggressively.

7. Ardashir I's Later Reign and Achievements

Having taken the throne around 224 CE, Ardashir spent the next decade consolidating his gains and refining his administrative structure. By the early 230s, he was recognized as the uncontested ruler of a region spanning from the Euphrates to eastern Iran—roughly the same territory that the Parthians had once held.

Fortifying the Empire

Ardashir ordered the building or improvement of **city walls** and frontier fortresses, especially in vulnerable areas near Rome or in the northeast, where nomadic raids posed a risk. He also reformed the military, ensuring that local troops were commanded by officers loyal to the crown. Heavy cavalry units continued to be the backbone of the army, but Ardashir introduced more advanced siege techniques, possibly influenced by Roman methods.

Encouraging Trade

Despite the tighter central grip, Ardashir recognized the economic benefits of trade. Merchants from India, China, and the Roman

Empire traversed the Silk Road, passing through Persian lands. Ardashir promised them better security, reducing the risk of bandit attacks or local tolls. This brought **new wealth** into the royal treasury. Some of these funds were used to sponsor public works—roads, bridges, and irrigation systems—that further strengthened the empire's stability.

Succession Plans

To avoid the constant strife that had plagued the Parthians, Ardashir designated **Shapur I**, his son, as his heir during his own lifetime. He gave Shapur important commands and placed him in charge of campaigns, ensuring he had both military experience and political clout. By making this arrangement public, Ardashir aimed to prevent disputes upon his death.

Though minor revolts and border troubles continued, Ardashir's policies created a firmer base for the empire than had existed under the later Parthian kings. By the time he died (likely around 241 CE), the empire was on stable footing—ready for his son to take it to greater heights.

---

8. A New Era for Persia

Ardashir I's reign marks a **turning point** in Persian history:

- **Restoration of Strong Monarchy**: Where Parthian kings had wrestled with endless noble rivalries, Ardashir planted the idea of a more absolute kingship, supported by religion and heritage.
- **Cultural Renaissance**: By invoking ancient Persian symbols and promoting a rejuvenated Zoroastrian structure, Ardashir encouraged an imperial culture that merged old and new, forging a sense of unity across diverse populations.

- **Shift in Regional Power**: Rome now faced a more centralized and ambitious rival in the East. While the Parthians had sometimes played defense, the Sasanians soon went on the offensive under Shapur I and his successors.

Even though the Sasanian Empire inherited many Parthian customs—especially in its cavalry-based military—its method of governance differed by emphasizing a more centralized bureaucracy and a clearer link between throne and temple.

---

9. Legacy of Ardashir I

When historians reflect on Ardashir I, they often credit him with **establishing the Sasanian Empire's core institutions**. He laid down a model of kingship that his descendants would refine. Key aspects of his legacy include:

Administrative Foundations
Ardashir's approach to provincial governance gave the Sasanians a more stable apparatus than the Parthians had. This structure, with its organized taxation and overseers, lasted throughout the Sasanian era, though it evolved under later kings.

Zoroastrian Patronage
His partnership with the priesthood had far-reaching effects, shaping religious policy for centuries. While this closeness brought unity, it also spurred religious debates and, at times, intolerance toward other faiths in later periods.

Military Readiness
Ardashir proved that the Iranian cavalry tradition could be adapted and improved. Under him, the empire learned from Rome's siege tactics and possibly from other neighboring powers, creating an army that was flexible enough to defend or expand.

Ideological Clarity

By openly claiming the heritage of the Achaemenids, Ardashir gave the Sasanian Empire a **grand sense of identity**. This made the empire attractive to Iranian nobles who felt pride in a restored Persian monarchy. It also gave Roman observers a jolt, as they realized they faced not just another petty state, but an empire with centuries-old claims of grandeur.

Although Ardashir I's reign lasted only about 15 to 17 years after he toppled the Parthians, he achieved a transformation that would shape the region for the next four centuries—until the early Islamic conquests of the 7th century CE.

CHAPTER 15

SHAPUR I AND THE EARLY SASANIAN STRENGTH

Introduction

In our previous chapter, we saw how Ardashir I defeated the last Parthian king and founded the Sasanian Empire. He worked quickly to bring the provinces of Iran and Mesopotamia under a more centralized rule, set up a stronger administrative system, and allied himself closely with Zoroastrian priests. By the time of Ardashir's death (around 241 CE), the new empire was already on solid ground, yet it was still young, with much consolidation and expansion ahead.

Now, in Chapter 15, we turn our focus to **Shapur I**, Ardashir I's son and successor. Shapur I played a major role in shaping the character of the early Sasanian Empire, building on his father's accomplishments and adding his own stamp of authority. During his reign (c. 240–270 CE, though exact dates vary), he confronted the Roman Empire in a series of daring campaigns, recorded memorable victories, and captured a Roman emperor—the only time in history that happened. He also oversaw significant building projects, supported religious movements (including some that stirred controversy), and helped refine the empire's bureaucracy.

In this chapter, we will explore how Shapur I established himself as a powerful ruler, examine his famous wars against Rome, and learn about the social, cultural, and religious developments that took place under his rule. By the end, we will see how the Sasanian Empire transformed from Ardashir's new dynasty into a formidable power recognized across the Near East and beyond.

1. Shapur I's Rise to the Throne

While Ardashir I still lived, he made it clear that **Shapur I** was to be his heir. Ardashir granted Shapur leadership roles in the military and administration, ensuring that he was widely respected by nobles and provincial governors. When Ardashir died (around 241 CE), there was little challenge to Shapur's succession—very different from the succession wars that had plagued the later Parthian era.

Key points about Shapur's background:

Experience in Campaigns
Even before taking the throne, Shapur participated in military expeditions to secure border regions, such as campaigns in the east against local tribes. This hands-on experience gave him practical knowledge of warfare and won him the loyalty of the armies.

Connection to Zoroastrian Priests
Like his father, Shapur recognized the importance of religious support. He maintained strong ties with Zoroastrian priests, continuing the practice of royal involvement in temple affairs and upholding the notion that the king's authority was linked to divine approval.

Desire for Expansion
Shapur inherited a stable empire, but he also had ambitions to extend Sasanian influence beyond what Ardashir had achieved. In particular, he saw Rome to the west as both a threat and an opportunity: defeating Roman armies could bring glory, wealth, and possibly new territories.

With these foundations, Shapur I began his reign with confidence. The question was not whether he would continue his father's policies, but rather **how boldly** he would push forward.

2. Early Reign: Consolidation and Diplomacy

Shapur I began by consolidating Sasanian control in the core provinces. Although Ardashir had subdued the main centers of resistance, some local lords still needed reminders of who was in charge.

Securing Mesopotamia
Mesopotamia, with its fertile lands and important trade routes, was crucial. Shapur stationed trustworthy generals and administrators in the region to ensure taxes and resources flowed smoothly. He also improved the defenses around major cities such as **Ctesiphon** and **Seleucia**, anticipating possible conflicts with Rome.

Managing Eastern Territories
On the empire's eastern front, Shapur continued or concluded campaigns against smaller dynasties and tribal groups along the Oxus River (Amu Darya) or in regions like Sistan. These campaigns had two objectives:

- **To prevent** any rival from rising and challenging Sasanian authority.
- **To maintain** secure borders that would allow him to focus on the west without worrying about sudden raids from the east.

Relations with the Nobility
Following Ardashir's model, Shapur sought to balance noble power by rewarding loyalty while also rotating key offices among different families. For instance, he might place a governor from one prominent house in a province but select the military commander from another, preventing any single family from growing too strong.

Though these measures were not revolutionary, they helped maintain a stable internal structure at a time when Shapur was already looking outward, particularly toward Rome.

3. The Road to War with Rome

Since the days of the Parthians, relations with Rome had often involved skirmishes over Armenia and Mesopotamia. The new Sasanian regime, led by Ardashir and then Shapur, inherited these tensions. Roman armies remained stationed near the Euphrates, and Roman client kings held sway in border regions. Shapur saw potential not just to defend but to **go on the offensive** and prove the Sasanians a stronger force than the Parthians had been.

Early Clashes under Ardashir and Shapur
During Ardashir's final years, there were minor confrontations with Roman garrisons near the Euphrates. Shapur participated in these, gaining insight into Roman tactics. He concluded that Roman forces, while disciplined, could be vulnerable if caught in difficult terrain or faced with swift cavalry maneuvers.

State of Rome
Around the mid-3rd century CE, the Roman Empire was experiencing its own difficulties—often called the **Crisis of the Third Century**. Emperors rose and fell quickly, civil wars erupted, and pressures on multiple frontiers drained Roman resources. Shapur sensed an opportunity: a weakened Rome might be easier to defeat, or at least to push out of contested areas like Armenia and Mesopotamia.

Strategic Ambitions
Shapur's goals were not only military. Controlling more of Mesopotamia, including cities like Antioch (in modern Turkey), would grant the Sasanian Empire significant economic and strategic advantages. He might also aim to establish buffer zones or client states that recognized Sasanian authority, reducing Rome's ability to mount invasions.

These factors combined to lay the groundwork for Shapur's first major campaigns against the Roman Empire, which would become a defining feature of his rule.

4. The First War: Successes and Setbacks

Shapur's initial foray into Roman territories likely began in the early 240s CE. He advanced into **Roman Mesopotamia**, capturing or intimidating local cities.

Capture of Hatra?

Some sources suggest Shapur targeted **Hatra**, a desert fortress city that had held off past invaders, including Romans and possibly Parthians. If he managed to subdue Hatra, it would be a symbolic and strategic gain, as Hatra's formidable walls had repelled many previous assaults. The details are murky, but it appears Shapur succeeded in either capturing or neutralizing this key outpost.

Pressure on Roman Garrison Towns

Roman-controlled towns such as **Nisibis** and **Edessa** found themselves threatened or besieged. Shapur's cavalry likely circled these areas, cutting off supplies and forcing negotiations. Even if he did not fully capture every fortress, his raids disrupted Roman lines and showcased Sasanian strength.

Roman Response

The Roman Emperor at the time was **Gordian III** (reigned 238–244 CE), a young ruler guided by senior advisers. Hearing of Shapur's advances, Gordian III mobilized a large force to push the Sasanians back. A significant engagement occurred near **Resaena** in 243 CE, where Gordian III claimed victory, at least temporarily halting Shapur's penetration.

However, Gordian III died under unclear circumstances in 244 CE (some sources suggest a mutiny), and his successor **Philip the Arab** signed a peace treaty with Shapur. In that treaty, Rome may have paid an indemnity or recognized certain Sasanian gains in Mesopotamia. This outcome was a **propaganda win** for Shapur, who boasted that Rome's new emperor had effectively conceded to Sasanian might.

Despite these successes, Shapur had not destroyed Rome's eastern armies. He had proven, though, that the Sasanian Empire was not to be trifled with, and that it could dictate terms under certain conditions.

---

5. The Second War and the Famous Capture of Valerian

Perhaps the most dramatic episode of Shapur's reign—and indeed a landmark in ancient history—was the **capture of the Roman Emperor Valerian**. It happened in the 260s CE and caused a sensation throughout the Mediterranean world.

Renewed Conflict
After Philip the Arab's reign, new Roman emperors emerged as the empire sank further into the **Crisis of the Third Century**. Valerian took power in 253 CE and attempted to restore stability. By the late 250s, Shapur was again pushing Roman frontiers, possibly capturing Antioch (a major city) and other settlements in Syria. Valerian marched east with a large force, determined to end the Sasanian threat.

The Battle and Valerian's Defeat
In 260 CE, near a place traditionally identified as **Edessa** (though details vary), Shapur's army engaged Valerian's forces. Through a combination of skillful cavalry tactics, strategic positioning, and perhaps disarray in the Roman ranks, the Sasanians overwhelmed Valerian's army. Valerian himself was **taken prisoner**—the first and only time a Roman emperor was captured alive by a foreign enemy.

Implications of the Capture

Shapur paraded Valerian around as a trophy of war, using him and other Roman prisoners for propaganda. Several rock reliefs still visible in Iran show Shapur on horseback, triumphantly receiving Valerian's submission. Roman sources offer grim tales of Valerian's later fate, though these accounts may be exaggerated. Regardless, the capture shocked the Roman world, showing just how fragile its imperial leadership had become.

From Shapur's perspective, this event cemented his reputation as a **conqueror**. He gained loot, slaves, and engineers among the prisoners, some of whom he used to build grand projects in Persia. Valerian's capture also demoralized many Roman provinces in the East, which fell under temporary or partial Sasanian influence.

Still, Shapur did not attempt a permanent occupation of the entire Roman East. He likely understood that holding vast tracts of enemy territory would strain his resources. Instead, he withdrew with plunder and captives, leaving a power vacuum that local rulers filled. Rome would eventually regroup under leaders like Odaenathus of Palmyra and later Emperor Aurelian, but for a time, Shapur stood as the victor.

---

6. Administration, Projects, and Cultural Achievements Under Shapur

Military success was not Shapur's only focus. He also took steps to **strengthen the empire's internal workings** and foster cultural development.

Use of Captive Labor

A significant outcome of Shapur's wars was the influx of Roman prisoners of war, including skilled artisans and engineers. Shapur put them to work on major construction and infrastructure projects. These included:

- **Roads**: Improving or creating trade routes to help caravan traffic move more smoothly and quickly.
- **Bridges and Canals**: Especially along the Tigris and Euphrates, aiding agriculture and commerce.
- **New Cities**: Shapur reportedly founded or refounded certain cities, such as **Bishapur** (in southern Iran), blending Roman and Persian architectural styles.

Royal Patronage of Religions
Like his father, Shapur was a supporter of Zoroastrianism. However, during Shapur's time, other religious movements also gained footing. For instance, **Manichaeism**, founded by the prophet Mani, spread in these years. Mani claimed to bring a universal truth, combining elements of Zoroastrianism, Christianity, and Buddhism. Shapur I offered Mani some degree of patronage—at least for a time—likely intrigued by the notion of bridging different faiths under one empire.

This willingness to sponsor Mani's teachings shows that, while the Sasanians promoted Zoroastrianism, there was initially some openness to religious diversity. That said, the main priests of Zoroastrianism remained deeply influential in the court, so Shapur had to balance support for Mani with the interests of traditional magi.

Refining Bureaucracy
Under Shapur, the Sasanian administrative system continued to evolve. He built on Ardashir's foundations by refining tax policies, making them more predictable. He encouraged local governors to keep standardized records and to report directly to the royal chancery in the capital region (Ctesiphon). This centralized approach reduced the chance of local revolts or excessive autonomy among nobles.

At the same time, Shapur allowed many local customs to remain intact. Provinces could use their own languages or traditions for minor matters, as long as they recognized the overarching Sasanian authority. This blend of central control with local flexibility became a hallmark of successful Sasanian governance.

7. The Later Years of Shapur's Reign

After the capture of Valerian in 260 CE, Shapur reigned for roughly another decade. This period saw continued efforts to maintain the empire's prosperity and to fend off any Roman counterattacks.

Threats from Palmyra

Palmyra, a wealthy city-state in the Syrian Desert, rose in power under the leadership of **Odaenathus**, who managed to rally local forces, including Roman remnants, to push Sasanian troops out of certain territories. Odaenathus actually took the title of "King of Kings" in the East, attempting to form a buffer state under nominal Roman authority. He inflicted defeats on Sasanian garrisons, showing that Shapur's hold on conquered lands was not unassailable.

Defensive Measures and Diplomacy

Shapur responded by reinforcing eastern Syria and Mesopotamia, but he did not commit to a full-scale war against Palmyra. Some historians suggest he may have tried to negotiate or was content to maintain a status quo, focusing on internal empire-building rather than endless war.

Over time, Rome stabilized under emperors like Aurelian, who defeated Palmyra and gradually reasserted Roman influence. While Shapur still held onto important strongholds and had not lost face, the days of dramatic Sasanian advances into Roman territory wound down as the empire turned inward for consolidation.

Succession Planning

As Shapur grew older, the question of who would follow him became more pressing. Some sources mention different sons contending for favor. Ultimately, a prince named **Hormizd** (Hormizd I) appeared poised to succeed, though other princes also held important positions. Before Shapur's death (around 270 CE), he likely worked to ensure a smooth transition, recalling how critical a stable succession had been to Sasanian success so far.

Shapur I's reign thus ended on a note of relative stability. Though he faced challenges at the frontier, he had embedded the Sasanian Empire in the region's geopolitical landscape as a force comparable—or sometimes superior—to Rome.

8. Assessing Shapur I's Impact

Shapur I's long reign left a deep imprint on the Sasanian Empire. Several key points stand out:

Military Prestige

Shapur brought the Sasanians to the height of their martial reputation by defeating multiple Roman emperors, most notably capturing Valerian. This feat reverberated across the ancient world, proving that the new Persian dynasty could match and even exceed the achievements of the old Parthians.

Consolidation of Empire

Inside the empire, Shapur continued the work of centralizing authority, streamlining administration, and building infrastructure. This laid a firmer groundwork for his successors to sustain a stable state that could handle foreign threats and internal governance more effectively than the Parthians had.

Cultural and Religious Developments

By welcoming skilled artisans and laborers from abroad—whether Roman captives or others—Shapur encouraged a fusion of artistic styles. At the same time, he allowed religious thinkers like Mani a space to operate, at least initially, reflecting a certain curiosity about bridging diverse traditions. However, the magi's dominance in court life also grew, setting the stage for more stringent Zoroastrian orthodoxy in the future.

Limits of Expansion

Despite his successes, Shapur did not attempt to fully conquer or permanently hold large portions of the Roman Empire. Instead, he focused on strategic points, plunder, and maintaining a buffer zone. This was likely a practical decision to avoid overextending Sasanian resources. Yet it also showed that while the Sasanians were formidable, they did not aim to replicate the Achaemenid Empire's vast conquests in the West; controlling the core Iranian plateau and nearby regions effectively was enough to secure their power.

In sum, Shapur I stands as one of the most remarkable Sasanian kings, forging a legacy of both war and state-building that future rulers would try to emulate or adapt.

---

9. Conclusion of Chapter 15

Shapur I took over from his father Ardashir I and transformed the newly founded Sasanian Empire into a genuine great power of the 3rd century CE. By defeating Roman armies and capturing an emperor, he showed the world that the Sasanians were not merely successors to the Parthians—they were an ambitious, well-organized state with a capable military and a unifying imperial ideology. At home, Shapur consolidated control, developed cities, and engaged with religious figures like Mani, further shaping Persian culture and governance.

Under Shapur's rule, the Sasanian Empire stood on equal footing with its western rival, Rome, and even surpassed it at times. As we will see in the next chapter, the internal stability and prestige Shapur built would allow his successors to continue in a similar vein—though they would also face new challenges and shifting dynamics. In **Chapter 16**, we will explore the broader **Golden Age of the Sasanian Empire**, when artistic, economic, and military achievements flourished, but also when tensions with Rome and internal religious debates grew more intense. This era set many precedents that would shape the Middle East for centuries.

CHAPTER 16

THE GOLDEN AGE OF THE SASANIAN EMPIRE

Introduction

We have followed the story of the Sasanian Empire from its founding under Ardashir I to its rise under Shapur I, who made a dramatic impact by capturing the Roman Emperor Valerian and consolidating Sasanian rule. Now, in Chapter 16, we delve into what many historians refer to as the "Golden Age" of the Sasanian Empire—a period that spans roughly the late 3rd to early 5th centuries CE.

During this time, the empire reached new heights of **cultural, economic, and military power**. Sasanian art and architecture blended Iranian traditions with influences from Mesopotamia, Rome, and beyond, creating a distinctive style that impressed neighbors and later generations alike. Trade routes flourished, linking East and West through Persian lands. Kings such as Hormizd I, Bahram I, Narseh, Yazdegerd I, and Bahram V built on Shapur's foundations, each contributing to the empire's stability or expansion in different ways.

Yet this era was not without challenges: internal religious controversies grew, especially as Zoroastrian priests sought a more uniform orthodoxy, sometimes clashing with Christian and other minority faiths. Relations with Rome (and later Byzantium) continued in cycles of war and peace. By examining this "Golden Age," we see how the Sasanians tried to balance tradition and innovation, forging a realm that left a profound legacy on Iranian identity and the broader region.

1. Succession After Shapur I

When Shapur I died around 270 CE, the Sasanian throne did not automatically pass smoothly. Different sources mention a variety of short-lived rulers—some say Hormizd I, others mention a brief rule by Bahram I. The historical record is murky, but eventually, the empire settled under a series of kings who, while not as individually famous as Shapur I, collectively maintained Sasanian power.

Hormizd I (r. 270-271 CE)
Called "Hormizd the Brave" in some texts, Hormizd I seems to have had a short reign. He was likely a capable military leader under Shapur but did not hold the throne long enough to implement major reforms. Still, the continuity of Shapur's policies helped maintain stability.

Bahram I and Bahram II
These rulers appear to have focused on internal governance, dealing with ongoing tensions in the eastern provinces and religious disputes at court. Bahram II, for instance, faced renewed Roman pressure. The legendary Roman Emperor Carus invaded Mesopotamia around 283 CE and might have briefly threatened Ctesiphon before Carus's sudden death halted the campaign.

Narseh (r. c. 293-302 CE)
Narseh, another son of Shapur I (according to some accounts), challenged Bahram III in a brief succession struggle. Once in power, Narseh proved an effective ruler, reorganizing provinces and confronting the Roman Empire again. In 296 CE, he fought Emperor Galerius but suffered a defeat, leading to a treaty that cost the Sasanians some territory. Despite this setback, Narseh maintained Sasanian dominance in the core lands.

By the early 4th century, the throne passed through the hands of several kings, but the system set in place by Ardashir and Shapur endured. The empire did not fracture into civil wars as the Parthian realm had. Instead, it continued to move forward, albeit with some bumps.

---

2. Economic Prosperity and Trade Routes

One hallmark of the Sasanian Golden Age was the empire's thriving economy. **Trade** served as the lifeblood of Sasanian wealth, connecting the Mediterranean world with Central Asia, India, and even China.

Control of the Silk Road
The famous Silk Road, or rather the network of routes known by that name, passed through Persia on its way from China to the Levant. By ensuring relative safety for caravans, the Sasanian authorities collected taxes on goods like silk, spices, metals, and precious stones. These taxes filled the royal treasury and funded grand building projects.

Maritime Links
In addition to overland routes, the Sasanians developed maritime trade in the Persian Gulf and the Indian Ocean. Ports along the southern coast of Iran linked with Indian and East African traders. This seaborne commerce brought products like pearls, ivory, and exotic woods.

Urban Growth
Cities flourished as commercial hubs, particularly in Mesopotamia. Towns like Ctesiphon, Gundeshapur, and Bishapur became centers of craft production—textiles, metalwork, pottery—often mixing local Persian styles with influences from Greek or Roman artistry. The result was a **blended culture** that appealed to diverse merchants passing through.

This vibrant economy supported the empire's military campaigns, financed public works, and elevated the standard of living for many city dwellers—though, of course, peasants in outlying areas still faced the hard realities of agricultural life.

---

3. Sasanian Art, Architecture, and Cultural Flourishing

The Sasanian era is known for its distinctive **visual and architectural achievements**. Artists and builders combined older Iranian traditions with new ideas, leading to a style that future Persian dynasties would admire and emulate.

Palaces and Rock Reliefs

Following Shapur I's example, subsequent kings commissioned **rock reliefs** in places like Naqsh-e Rostam and Naqsh-e Rajab, depicting royal victories or ceremonial scenes. These reliefs often featured a frontal view of the king in ornate attire, receiving homage from courtiers or gods.

Grand palaces also sprang up in cities and royal estates. These structures commonly included **iwans**—large vaulted halls open on one side—an architectural form that became a hallmark of Persian design.

Metalwork and Decorative Arts

Sasanian craftsmen excelled in **silver plate** production, creating elaborate dishes and bowls decorated with hunting scenes, mythological figures, or stylized plant motifs. These items became prized exports and diplomatic gifts, spreading Sasanian artistic influence widely.

Literature and Scholarship

While much of the Sasanian written tradition has been lost, we know that **Zoroastrian priests** compiled religious texts during this period, and that Persian scholars engaged with Greek, Indian, and other bodies of knowledge. The city of **Gundeshapur** in southwestern Iran hosted a renowned academy, where medicine, astronomy, philosophy, and other fields were studied—a precursor to later Islamic Golden Age centers of learning.

By fostering a climate of cultural creativity, the Sasanians reinforced their image as refined monarchs, not merely warlords. This cultural legacy would resonate through later Iranian history, even after the empire's fall.

---

4. Religious Debates and the Growth of Orthodoxy

One of the major shifts in the Sasanian Golden Age was the consolidation of **Zoroastrianism** as a more formal state religion—though not without contention.

Rise of the Zoroastrian Priesthood

During this period, high priests, sometimes called the **Mobedan Mobed** (chief priest), gained prominence. They lobbied for a standardized form of Zoroastrian worship and theology, codifying rituals and texts. Kings who supported this process benefited from the priesthood's public endorsement, further legitimizing their rule.

Suppression of Other Faiths?

As Zoroastrianism grew in official standing, some kings tolerated religious diversity, while others enacted harsh measures against groups deemed heretical or dangerous. For instance, under Bahram I, the prophet Mani was reportedly imprisoned and died in captivity—signaling a turn against Manichaeism. Later on, **Christianity** also faced periods of persecution, especially when relations with the Christian Byzantine Empire deteriorated.

However, the level of persecution varied by reign. Some monarchs, like Yazdegerd I (r. 399–420 CE), took a more tolerant stance, earning both praise and criticism. In general, the trend was toward a closer bond between throne and fire altar—an attempt to unify the empire under a single religious identity.

Impact on Society

Over time, the Zoroastrian establishment gained control over marriage laws, inheritance, and moral policing. This heightened religious dimension shaped social norms, especially regarding purity, family structures, and festivals like **Nowruz**. While large segments of the population found these regulations acceptable or even beneficial, minority communities sometimes struggled under laws that favored Zoroastrians in legal disputes or tax exemptions.

5. Military Evolution and Conflicts with Rome/Byzantium

Although the Sasanian Empire engaged in wars throughout its history, the Golden Age saw the development of more advanced military structures. The cavalry remained dominant, but new strategies emerged in response to changes in the Roman Empire, which, by the 4th century CE, had evolved into the **Byzantine Empire** in the East.

Heavy Cavalry and Siege Warfare

Sasanian kings recognized the need for improved **siege engines**, including battering rams and siege towers, especially in campaigns against well-fortified Byzantine cities. Their engineers learned from captured Romans or mercenaries, refining catapults and other devices to breach strongholds.

Border Fortifications

Along the Euphrates and in the Caucasus region, the Sasanians built or upgraded fortresses to keep Roman/Byzantine forces at bay. Sometimes these fortifications were part of negotiated buffer zones. Other times, they formed the front line when truces failed.

Cycles of War and Diplomacy

Relations with Rome/Byzantium in this era frequently followed a **pattern**: a Sasanian king or a Byzantine emperor saw an opportunity or provocation, launched an invasion, seized some fortresses or plunder, and then both sides negotiated peace. This pattern repeated itself over the centuries. Battles might occur in Armenia, Mesopotamia, or the Caucasus, with each power aiming to force the other into a favorable treaty.

Despite these conflicts, trade and cultural exchange continued. Diplomatic marriages sometimes occurred. Embassies traveled between Ctesiphon and Constantinople, exchanging gifts and occasionally forging short-lived alliances against mutual enemies (like nomadic groups threatening the Caucasus).

6. Notable Kings of the Golden Age

While a complete list of Sasanian kings is lengthy, a few stand out during this generally prosperous period:

Yazdegerd I (r. 399–420 CE)
Known by some as "Yazdegerd the Sinner" (due to criticism by conservative Zoroastrian priests) and by others as a just ruler, Yazdegerd I tried to ease tensions with the Byzantine Empire and showed relative tolerance toward Christians. He also balanced noble power by appointing loyal men to key positions, but this policy garnered hostility from certain aristocratic factions.

Bahram V (r. 420–438 CE)
Often remembered in Persian literature as **Bahram Gur**—"Gur" referring to the onager or wild ass that he famously hunted—Bahram V became a cultural icon. Stories portray him as a romantic and chivalrous king, though the historical record indicates he also conducted military campaigns, maintaining Sasanian strength. He upheld Zoroastrian orthodoxy but did not fully repress minority faiths, apparently preferring a balanced approach.

Yazdegerd II and Beyond
Successors like Yazdegerd II (r. 438–457 CE) and Peroz I (r. 457–484 CE) faced new challenges, including conflicts with the **Hephthalites** (a nomadic people east of Iran) and shifting alliances with the Byzantines. While the empire remained strong, these rulers had to work harder to contain threats on multiple fronts.

Overall, these kings contributed to the empire's golden reputation through effective governance, cultural patronage, and generally stable borders—though cracks began to appear, especially from nomadic incursions in the northeast.

7. Social Stratification and Daily Life

Beneath the royal splendor and monumental architecture lay a complex social structure that influenced **daily life** in the Sasanian Empire. Society was broadly divided into classes:

The Royal Family and Nobles
At the top were the **Shahanshah** and his relatives, followed by a tier of great noble houses. These nobles held large estates, commanded private armies, and often served as provincial governors or high-ranking court officials.

Priesthood
Zoroastrian priests (magi) formed a distinct influential group. They oversaw religious rituals, managed temple lands, and advised the king on moral and legal matters. Over time, they gained a firm grip on spiritual and, in some cases, judicial authority.

Commoners and Artisans
City dwellers included craftsmen, merchants, and laborers. Many artisans were engaged in textile production (fabrics, carpets), metalwork, or pottery. Trade hubs like Ctesiphon and Nishapur had lively markets where people from different ethnicities—Arameans, Greeks, Jews, Syrians, Arabs—mingled.

Peasants
The majority lived in rural areas, farming wheat, barley, fruits, and raising livestock. Some were tenants on noble estates, paying rent or taxes in produce. Their lives were often dominated by agricultural cycles, local feudal obligations, and the demands of the state or landlord.

The monarchy tried to keep this social order stable, enacting laws to define each class's rights and responsibilities. Marriage laws, inheritance rules, and moral codes often reflected Zoroastrian principles as interpreted by the priesthood.

8. Religious Minorities and Cultural Exchange

Despite the growing hold of Zoroastrian orthodoxy, the Sasanian Empire was home to many religious communities:

Christians
Christian communities, especially in Mesopotamia, thrived under certain kings who allowed them to build churches and run schools. However, during periods of war with the Christian Byzantine Empire, Christians in Persian lands could be seen as potential fifth columnists, leading to persecution.

Jews
A long-established Jewish population lived in Babylonian territories, continuing traditions of scholarship that led to the creation of the **Babylonian Talmud** around this time. While relations with the Sasanian government varied, the Jewish community often found more stability here than under Roman or Byzantine rule, as they were not religious rivals in the same way Christians were.

Manichaeans and Other Groups
After Mani's death, Manichaeism spread along the Silk Road, despite official crackdowns. Some Sasanian regions turned a blind eye to smaller sects, allowing them to exist if they paid taxes and did not challenge state authority.

This patchwork of faiths enriched Sasanian culture, as ideas crossed boundaries in trade centers and intellectual circles, even if official policy sometimes leaned toward uniformity.

9. Shadows of Future Challenges

While the Golden Age brought prosperity and cultural brilliance, it also sowed seeds for future problems:

Increasing Power of Nobles and Priests
As the empire matured, certain noble families and high-ranking priests gained extensive wealth and local influence. If a king was weak, these elite factions could undermine his authority, leading to potential civil strife.

Byzantine Rivalry
The Roman Empire's evolution into the Christian Byzantine Empire introduced a new ideological dimension to their rivalry. By the 5th century, religious differences and competing claims over borderlands would lead to more frequent—and sometimes more b

Eastern Threats
Nomadic groups from Central Asia, like the **Hephthalites** (White Huns), pressed on the northeastern frontiers. Eventually, these groups would challenge the Sasanians in ways that tested their military resources severely, leading to defeats and internal fractures in later reigns.

For now, however, the Sasanian Empire still reaped the benefits of strong trade, a capable administration, and cultural unity—achievements that define this period as a golden era.

---

10. Conclusion of Chapter 16

The Golden Age of the Sasanian Empire stands as a time of **remarkable growth** in culture, economy, and statecraft. Building on the foundations laid by Ardashir I and Shapur I, successive kings refined administration, promoted grand artistic projects, and navigated the challenging waters of religious and social policy. They managed to keep the empire relatively unified and prosperous, even amid occasional wars with Rome/Byzantium.

This era's achievements—elaborate rock reliefs, thriving Silk Road commerce, strong cavalry forces, and a deepening link between monarchy and Zoroastrian priesthood—shaped Iranian identity for centuries. Yet we also see signs that the Sasanians would face rising difficulties: noble power blocs, fervent religious orthodoxy, external enemies in both West and East.

In our next chapters, we will see how the Sasanian Empire **contends with these growing pressures**, including more intense conflicts with Byzantium, shifts in internal politics, and the eventual challenges that lead to the empire's decline and fall. Through this, we gain insight into how even the most splendid golden ages rest on delicate balances that can be disrupted by changing times.

CHAPTER 17

WARS WITH ROME AND BYZANTIUM

Introduction

In the last chapter, we explored the Golden Age of the Sasanian Empire, a time when trade, art, and centralized governance flourished. Although the Sasanians often enjoyed prosperity, they also lived under the constant shadow of potential conflict with their western neighbor. The Roman Empire, which eventually evolved into the Byzantine Empire in the East, stood as a formidable rival that challenged Sasanian dominance in many areas. Wars, raids, and uneasy truces between these two powers lasted for centuries, forming a defining thread in Sasanian history.

In this chapter, we look closely at the long and complex struggles between the Sasanian rulers and the Roman (later Byzantine) emperors. We will see how each new generation inherited the ambitions, grudges, and border fortifications of the previous one, leading to repeated cycles of warfare along the Euphrates, in the Caucasus, and even into deeper territories. Diplomatic marriages, prisoner exchanges, and carefully negotiated treaties sometimes paused the fighting, but the rivalry rarely remained quiet for long. By understanding this persistent conflict, we also gain insight into how the Sasanians managed their army, balanced their resources, and adapted their strategies over time, all in hopes of securing a stable frontier and preserving the empire's prosperity.

The Legacy of Parthian-Roman Hostilities

The wars between the Sasanians and Rome did not begin in a vacuum. For centuries, the Parthians and Rome had fought over

Armenia and Mesopotamia. When Ardashir I founded the Sasanian Empire in the early third century CE, he inherited these disputes along with a sense of pride in challenging Roman armies. Shapur I, his successor, famously captured Emperor Valerian, which set an early tone that the Sasanian state could surpass even the best Roman legions. This achievement became a hallmark in the Sasanian imagination, shaping how future kings approached confrontation with Rome.

Yet despite early triumphs, the Sasanians discovered that Rome, and later Byzantium, was not easily subdued. The Romans had a long tradition of resilient logistics and strong fortifications. When pressed, they could draw on vast resources or shift armies from other frontiers, although internal crises sometimes constrained them. The Sasanians recognized that their best strategy was not always to try for permanent conquests but rather to maintain strong frontiers, seize opportunities when Rome was weak, and accept truces when faced with united Roman opposition.

Shifting from Rome to Byzantium

A major turning point came when Emperor Constantine the Great (r. 306–337 CE) founded Constantinople as the "New Rome" in the East and promoted Christianity as a state-favored religion. Over time, this transformed the Roman Empire into the Byzantine Empire in the eastern Mediterranean. The change to a Christian empire introduced a new ideological layer: conflicts were no longer purely territorial; they could also carry religious overtones, as a Zoroastrian power (the Sasanians) confronted a Christian power (Byzantium). When revolts or persecutions arose in borderlands where Christians or Zoroastrians lived, both sides used them as pretexts for interference, fueling deeper mistrust.

However, religious differences did not always mean total hostility. At various points, diplomacy served both empires well. They needed each other for trade and for containing threats from steppe nomads. The Byzantines learned to respect the Sasanian cavalry, and the Sasanians recognized Byzantine skill in siege warfare. The two empires coexisted in a love-hate relationship, each always ready to exploit the other's moment of weakness.

Notable Conflicts and Peace Treaties

Over the centuries, major wars erupted repeatedly. Rather than list them in bullet points, we can trace their general patterns and highlight a few key episodes.

In the fourth century, Shapur II (r. 309–379 CE) led sustained campaigns against Rome. Early in his reign, he faced internal pressures, but once established, he turned west. Shapur II is often credited with reorganizing the Sasanian military to better handle sieges, adopting advanced siege engines and tunnels. He besieged the fortress of Nisibis multiple times, though the city's Roman defenders held out. Despite failing to take Nisibis, Shapur II gained a reputation for pushing deep into Roman territory and for his strong stance against Christian influence within his domain, possibly as a reaction to the Christian empire he fought in the West.

A significant treaty in this era was made between the Emperor Jovian and Shapur II around 363 CE, after the Roman Emperor Julian had failed in a campaign against the Sasanians and lost his life. Jovian, desperate to save the Roman army, agreed to cede key fortresses and lands, granting Shapur II notable gains in Mesopotamia. This accord proved that the Sasanians could force Rome to negotiate from a position of weakness if circumstances aligned.

In the fifth century, Yazdegerd I (r. 399–420 CE) and Bahram V (r. 420–438 CE) often sought peaceful relations with Byzantium, though occasional clashes broke out. Yazdegerd I, known for a more tolerant approach, sometimes acted as a mediator for Christians under Byzantine rule. Meanwhile, Bahram V's era saw smaller-scale conflicts that tested the frontiers, but neither side committed fully to an all-out war. When major tensions rose, both empires often found it preferable to sign a truce and focus on internal matters.

The sixth century brought renewed intensity. The Emperor Justinian (r. 527–565) tried to restore Roman glory, building magnificent architecture in Constantinople and reconquering parts of the old Western Empire. Meanwhile, the Sasanian throne passed through several rulers until it reached Khosrow I (also called Anushirvan, r. 531–579). Khosrow I admired wisdom and reform; he reorganized the tax system, refined the bureaucracy, and valued scholarship. Yet he also engaged in multiple wars with Justinian. These conflicts, often dubbed the Iberian or Lazic Wars, centered around the Caucasus region and the Black Sea coast. After bouts of fighting, the two empires signed the "Eternal Peace" treaty in 532 CE, which proved far from eternal. War resumed in the 540s and ended only after more negotiations, in which Khosrow I secured tribute payments from Justinian.

Khosrow I's reign marked a high point of Sasanian power, and Byzantium recognized him as a formidable opponent. When Khosrow I died, his successors continued to wrestle with Byzantium, though internal strife sometimes weakened the Sasanian effort. The final great Sasanian-Byzantine war erupted in the early seventh century under Khosrow II, leading to dramatic swings of fortune for both sides, which we will explore in later chapters.

Arms, Armor, and Strategy in the Prolonged Wars

The wars between the Sasanians and Rome (or Byzantium) spurred military innovation on both sides. The Sasanians depended heavily on their cavalry, known for swift archery and the fearsome charge of cataphracts, who wore heavy armor from head to toe. Over time, the Sasanian army also included more infantry equipped with spears, swords, or shields in a style partially influenced by their Western foes.

Byzantine armies benefited from strong defensive tactics, advanced fortifications, and the famed engineering tradition of the late Roman Empire. Siege warfare became a decisive element. Sasanians learned to build or adapt powerful siege engines for assaulting walled cities, but the Byzantines continually improved walls, moats, and watchtowers. Battles thus swung between swift cavalry raids in open country and protracted sieges of key strongholds.

Logistics played a vital role. The Euphrates and Tigris rivers served as supply lines or natural barriers. Whoever controlled the river crossings could gain a strategic edge. Both sides stationed garrisons along these rivers or in the Caucasus passes, forcing invaders to conduct lengthy sieges or rely on unprotected routes.

Economic considerations loomed as well. Sustaining armies for prolonged campaigns demanded heavy taxation, which could stir unrest at home. Emperors on both sides were careful to avoid bankrupting their treasuries. They sometimes settled for limited conquests or tributes rather than risking a total war that could destabilize their domains.

Diplomatic Maneuvers and Marriage Alliances

Even though war was frequent, there were times when Sasanians and Byzantines engaged in elaborate diplomacy. Envoys traveled back and forth, bearing letters and gifts. Each side tried to impress the other with courtly splendor while subtly probing for weaknesses. Discussions sometimes revolved around exchanging prisoners, delineating borders, or regulating trade routes.

Marriage alliances also appeared in rare instances. A Sasanian prince might marry a Byzantine princess, or vice versa, to seal a peace treaty. These unions often faced skepticism from religious authorities, since a Christian marrying into a Zoroastrian monarchy (or the other way around) raised many concerns. Yet the possibility of forging a stable alliance sometimes overcame these qualms, at least momentarily. Still, such marriages rarely ended the deep rivalry that shaped each empire's identity.

Civil Strife and Leadership Changes

Both empires suffered from internal crises that influenced their wars. The Sasanians faced noble revolts or contested successions. The Byzantines grappled with political intrigue in Constantinople, sometimes resulting in assassinations or rebellions. When one empire fell into chaos, the other might exploit the moment by attacking frontiers or demanding tribute.

An example emerged when the Byzantine Emperor Phocas (r. 602–610) took power in a coup that deposed his predecessor Maurice. Khosrow II (r. 590–628) used this event to claim he was acting on behalf of the slain Emperor Maurice's family. Khosrow II launched a massive invasion, exploiting Byzantine internal turmoil to seize large portions of the Near East, including Syria, Palestine, and even reaching Egypt. For a moment, it appeared the Sasanians might restore an Achaemenid-level empire. The Byzantines, however, rallied under Emperor Heraclius, who led a daring counter-campaign. Eventually, he struck deep into the Sasanian heartland, forcing a collapse of Sasanian positions in the West. This late war left both powers exhausted, setting the stage for the Arab conquests that would soon sweep across the region.

Effects on Local Populations

The people living in the contested border regions, such as Armenia, Mesopotamia, and the Caucasus, often suffered most. Towns and farms changed hands repeatedly. Local chiefs or princes tried to align with whichever empire promised the best deal, only to be punished later if they switched sides. Civilians bore the brunt of sieges, heavy taxation, forced conscription, and occasional massacres.

Despite these hardships, some cities leveraged their position as frontier markets, selling supplies to whichever army arrived and profiting from trade caravans seeking safe passage. In Armenia, certain noble houses managed to preserve autonomy by skillfully balancing Roman/Byzantine and Sasanian demands. Others found themselves used as pawns in diplomatic or military gambits, with tragic results when trust was broken.

Ideological and Religious Undercurrents

Though wars between these two empires were driven by power politics, religious differences often sharpened hostility. The Byzantines saw themselves as defenders of Orthodox Christianity, and the Sasanians upheld Zoroastrian doctrines at court, although not all kings enforced strict orthodoxy. Furthermore, Christian communities flourished in parts of the Sasanian Empire, while Zoroastrian enclaves existed in Byzantine territory, creating tense cross-border dynamics.

Some Sasanian rulers used anti-Christian rhetoric to justify punishing regions suspected of pro-Byzantine sentiment. Conversely, Byzantine emperors sometimes portrayed their conflicts with the Sasanians as struggles against a "heathen" empire. Religious propaganda did not always dictate policy, but it contributed to a charged atmosphere in which each empire portrayed itself as the champion of the "true faith."

Consequences and Looking Ahead

Over centuries, the wars between the Sasanian Empire and Rome/Byzantium drained enormous resources. Neither side ever achieved a permanent, decisive conquest of the other's heartland. Instead, they fought to secure better frontiers, to gain prestige at home, or to protect allied states like Armenia. The cycle of battle, raid, and treaty became so ingrained that observers might have believed it would continue indefinitely.

Yet the final great conflict in the early seventh century under Khosrow II and Emperor Heraclius brought both empires to their knees. Cities lay in ruins, treasuries were empty, and populations were weary of endless war. When Arab armies arrived from the Arabian Peninsula in the mid-seventh century, they faced two exhausted superpowers. Both the Sasanian and Byzantine states struggled to muster effective resistance, and within a few decades, the entire political map of the Near East changed dramatically.

CHAPTER 18

THE LATER SASANIAN RULERS

Introduction

The Sasanian Empire, having reached its cultural and political zenith, found itself increasingly burdened by external wars and internal conflicts. In the previous chapter, we examined how the relentless struggles with Rome and Byzantium shaped the fortunes of the empire, draining resources and fueling a cycle of raids and treaties. Now, in Chapter 18, our attention shifts to the later Sasanian rulers who inherited the consequences of these prolonged wars.

We will see how successive kings tried to manage the powerful nobility, balance Zoroastrian orthodoxy with the presence of religious minorities, and protect the empire's frontiers from new threats like the Hephthalites. We will observe how some rulers, such as Kavad I and Khosrow I, attempted bold reforms and expansions, while others fell to noble conspiracies or faced short, turbulent reigns. By highlighting the internal challenges that arose in this final phase of Sasanian history, we gain a deeper appreciation of how a once-thriving empire found itself increasingly fragile, eventually leading toward collapse and conquest by Arab forces in the mid-seventh century.

After the Golden Age: Waning Stability

Although the Sasanian Empire maintained strong institutions, the system that had flourished in the "Golden Age" began to show signs of strain in the late fifth and early sixth centuries. Internal problems often derived from the very elements that had made the empire prosperous: a powerful noble class, a tight alliance with Zoroastrian clergy, and ambitions to dominate border regions.

Noble families, enriched by centuries of expansion, could rival the king's power in local regions. Priests, bolstered by the official status of Zoroastrianism, sometimes pressed for policies that alienated minority communities or demanded severe punishments for heresy. Meanwhile, the repeated conflicts with Byzantium and nomadic invasions in the east drained the treasury, requiring heavy taxation that burdened the peasantry. These pressures eroded the broad support that earlier kings had enjoyed.

Kavad I and the Rise of Khosrow I

One of the most notable later Sasanian rulers was Kavad I (r. 488–531 CE). Early in his reign, the empire faced a crisis from the Hephthalites, a nomadic group that seized portions of eastern Iran. Kavad also contended with a religious and social movement known as the Mazdakite movement, led by the reformer Mazdak. Mazdak preached a radical vision of social equality, communal sharing of property, and a reinterpretation of Zoroastrian teachings that threatened the established hierarchy. Some accounts claim that Kavad initially supported Mazdak or tolerated him to curb noble power, but eventually turned against the movement once he regained stability.

Kavad's rule was turbulent, with periods of exile and restoration. However, he managed to hold the empire together through alliances, carefully balancing the demands of priests, nobles, and commoners. Toward the end of his life, he positioned his favored son, Khosrow (later called Khosrow I Anushirvan), as heir. Khosrow I, ascending the throne in 531 CE, proved to be one of the most influential Sasanian monarchs since Shapur I.

Khosrow I (r. 531–579 CE) reorganized administration and finances, building on the experiences of earlier kings. He is remembered for his wise governance and interest in learning. Some historians believe Khosrow I invited Greek philosophers to his court after the Byzantine Emperor Justinian closed the Academy of Athens. He also engaged in further wars with Byzantium, as covered in the previous chapter, but often ended them with advantageous treaties. Khosrow I's reign is sometimes called a "Second Golden Age," though it was not free of conflict. It demonstrated that, with able leadership, the Sasanian system could still adapt and thrive.

Cracks in the System

Despite Khosrow I's achievements, the underlying tensions in Sasanian society did not vanish. Kings who followed had to confront a set of persistent problems. Noble families kept extensive estates, private armies, and networks of clients, all of which allowed them to challenge royal decrees if they wished. The priesthood demanded orthodoxy and could accuse kings or courtiers of impiety if their policies seemed too lenient toward other faiths. Economic demands, shaped by constant military readiness, led to heavier taxes, and rural communities bore that weight most directly.

Some rulers navigated these challenges with skill, others fell quickly. For example, Hormizd IV (r. 579–590 CE), son of Khosrow I, tried to continue his father's policies but faced revolts from the nobility. In a brutal twist, general Bahram Chobin rebelled, prompting the young prince Khosrow (later Khosrow II) to flee to Byzantine territory for help. These internal upheavals weakened the empire's unity. When Khosrow II retook the throne with Byzantine assistance, the arrangement seemed promising but carried a price: close cooperation with the foreign power he was supposed to resist.

Khosrow II: A Final Flourish and Rapid Decline

Khosrow II (r. 590–628 CE) started his reign with the prestige of uniting the empire after a period of chaos. Eager to prove his strength, he waged a massive campaign against the Byzantine Empire when he felt they betrayed him. At first, he enjoyed staggering success. Sasanian armies took control of Syria, Palestine, and Egypt, capturing strategic cities like Damascus and Jerusalem, and even threatening Constantinople. For a brief moment, it seemed the Sasanians were on the verge of recreating the wide-ranging empire of ancient Achaemenid times.

However, the empire became overextended. Maintaining such distant possessions required huge numbers of troops, long supply lines, and stable governance at home. The Byzantines found a dynamic leader in Emperor Heraclius, who launched a counteroffensive directly into the Sasanian heartland. By striking near the Tigris and Euphrates, Heraclius forced Khosrow II to retreat and defend his core provinces. The swift reversal left Sasanian frontiers in disarray, and Khosrow II's authority at court crumbled. A palace coup led to his removal and execution in 628 CE, plunging the empire into a deeper crisis.

Succession Struggles and Fading Power

After Khosrow II's fall, a rapid succession of rulers took the throne. Some lasted only months. Factions among the nobility and the priesthood jockeyed for control, each placing their preferred candidate on the throne. A few rulers, such as Queen Boran (daughter of Khosrow II), attempted reforms but lacked the broad support needed to restore unity. Plague, famine, and economic disruption worsened the turmoil.

Among the multiple claimants, none managed to replicate the strong leadership once shown by kings like Shapur I or Khosrow I. As the Sasanian regime weakened, armies deserted or disintegrated. The once-proud cavalry could not be maintained without stable financing and command structures. The nobility fought one another more than they defended the empire's frontiers. In this environment, outside threats grew bolder.

External Dangers on the Eastern and Southern Frontiers

While the Byzantines had been the classic foe to the west, a new power now emerged from the Arabian Peninsula. The early seventh century saw the rise of Islam under the Prophet Muhammad, uniting Arab tribes. After Muhammad's death in 632 CE, the Rashidun Caliphs led Arab armies on campaigns that extended far beyond the peninsula. For a brief time, the Sasanians might have dismissed these forces as minor raiders, but soon they realized these were disciplined and motivated armies with a unifying faith and leadership.

On the eastern side, the Hephthalites and other steppe groups remained a threat, though less pressing once the Sasanians struck alliances or containment strategies. Yet the empire could not handle multiple fronts simultaneously. The final blow would come from the south, in battles like Qadisiyyah (circa 636 CE) and Nahavand (642 CE), where Arab forces decisively defeated the Sasanian military. The disunity within the empire made a coordinated defense nearly impossible, and the Sasanian monarchy dissolved in the face of these losses.

Impact on Society and Culture

The later Sasanian rulers tried to maintain the splendors of their court traditions, but the ongoing wars and internal discord strained resources. Aristocratic families grew more independent, sometimes ignoring central directives. Zoroastrian priests worked to preserve their religious authority, yet found it challenging to enforce uniformity when the monarchy was too weak to back them firmly.

Ordinary people in rural areas or towns saw their lives disrupted by heavier taxes and conscription for wars that did not end in lasting victories. Some individuals turned to new faith movements, either out of spiritual conviction or in hopes of escaping oppression. The Christian population grew in certain regions, especially when local Sasanian officials softened policies in exchange for cooperation. Jewish communities remained vital in Babylonian centers, but they too navigated shifting alliances and rulers.

Despite these pressures, Iranian cultural forms, from art to architecture, continued to display creativity. Many of the final Sasanian kings still commissioned reliefs and palaces, though few matched the grandeur of earlier eras. Once the Arabs conquered the empire, much of the Sasanian bureaucratic and artistic legacy persisted, melding into the new Islamic civilization that arose in the region.

The Last Attempts at Reunification

In the final years, a few Sasanian loyalists attempted to rally around a monarch who could repel the Arab conquest. Yazdegerd III (r. 632–651 CE), believed to be the last crown prince of the Sasanian line, inherited a shattered realm. He tried to organize resistance, but local nobles were reluctant to give him absolute authority, and finances were depleted. The Arab armies, guided by caliphs in Medina or later Damascus, pressed forward methodically.

Yazdegerd III fled eastward, seeking refuge among regional governors who offered only lukewarm support. He was eventually killed in 651 CE, marking the symbolic end of the Sasanian monarchy. Some pockets of resistance lingered, but the empire as a cohesive entity was gone. Through these final attempts, it was clear that the greatest obstacle to a Sasanian revival was not only external invasion but also the deep internal fractures that had built up over decades.

Reflections on the Later Sasanian Legacy

Although the later Sasanian rulers presided over a period of decline, they also contributed lasting elements to Iranian civilization. Khosrow I's administrative and tax reforms had a long influence, shaping how local governors interacted with peasants and how revenues were gathered. Courtly culture, including music, poetry, and romance tales, flourished at times, setting the stage for future Persian literary traditions under Islamic dynasties.

The complexities of religious policy in this era prefigured some of the debates that would emerge under the new Islamic order, especially concerning how to treat minorities or unify diverse populations under a single creed. The fall of the empire did not erase Sasanian achievements; rather, many were absorbed into the fabric of the Caliphate, from coinage styles to official titles.

Despite the empire's collapse, the memory of Sasanian grandeur lived on, especially among Iranian scholars and national poets in later centuries. They drew on the stories of Ardashir, Shapur, and Khosrow I to celebrate an Iranian identity that bridged pre-Islamic and Islamic histories. Through epic poems like the Shahnameh, the later Sasanian rulers—both their triumphs and their tragedies—gained a legendary status that transcended their actual end.

CHAPTER 19

THE FALL OF THE SASANIAN EMPIRE

Introduction

In the previous chapters, we explored how later Sasanian rulers struggled to maintain power in a world marked by internal feuds and relentless wars with Byzantium. By the early seventh century, the empire had reached both a peak and a crisis under Khosrow II: vast conquests briefly recalled ancient Achaemenid glories, but the campaign overextended Sasanian resources. When Emperor Heraclius of Byzantium counterattacked deep into Persian lands, he shattered the confidence of the royal court, prompting coups and instability in Ctesiphon. In this chapter, we will focus on the final years of the Sasanian Empire. We will see how the rapid Arab conquests, driven by a newly united Islamic power, collided with a weakened realm still recovering from prolonged war and internal disunity. Although some Persian nobles tried to rally a defense, they found themselves confronted by an energetic foe and a fractious homeland. By 651 CE, the last vestiges of Sasanian royal authority had collapsed, ending more than four centuries of dynastic rule and forever altering the political map of the Near East.

The Aftermath of Khosrow II's Defeat

Khosrow II, whose armies had once marched through Syria and captured Jerusalem, ended his reign in humiliation. Overstretched by the long war with Byzantium, the Sasanian state could not sustain those distant conquests or defend the core lands against Heraclius's bold offensive. When Khosrow II faced internal revolts from nobles dissatisfied with his leadership, he was deposed and executed in 628 CE. This event triggered a new phase of chaos at court, since Khosrow II had executed many potential heirs, leaving the line of succession uncertain.

In the few years after 628 CE, multiple claimants emerged. Ardashir III, Khosrow's grandson, briefly held power, but other powerful figures like General Shahrbaraz seized Ctesiphon. Even some of Khosrow's daughters, such as Boran and Azarmidokht, took the throne, attempting to restore stability through reforms or peace overtures. Unfortunately, these short reigns did little to calm the empire. Factions of nobles and priests each wanted to preserve their own privileges, which only multiplied the succession struggles. By 632 CE, the monarchy's authority was so fractured that even loyal governors had trouble rallying under a single leader.

Amid this turmoil, the empire's finances were in shambles. The long war with Byzantium had drained the treasury, fields lay devastated in some regions, and trade routes remained insecure. Taxes rose, angering peasants and merchants. Zoroastrian priests tried to reassert order in local areas, but a sense of disillusionment spread among the population. The cohesive structure that had once allowed strong kings like Shapur I or Khosrow I to flourish was no longer in place, replaced by a swirl of court intrigues and regional power grabs.

The Emergence of the Arab Armies

While the Sasanian Empire tore itself apart, significant changes were under way in the Arabian Peninsula. The Prophet Muhammad's teachings had united many Arab tribes under the banner of Islam, forging a sense of shared identity and purpose. After Muhammad's death in 632 CE, the Rashidun Caliphs took the reins of leadership, aiming to expand Islam beyond Arabia. These caliphs oversaw well-disciplined armies driven by both religious zeal and promises of material gain. Their first major offensives pushed into Byzantine-held Syria and Sasanian-held Iraq, regions that were culturally and economically rich but also exhausted by constant warfare.

The timing proved decisive. Byzantium, although battered by the recent war, still managed some resistance in Syria. However, the Sasanians were in far worse shape, lacking a strong monarch or a united command structure. The earliest Arab raids into southern Mesopotamia revealed just how vulnerable Persia had become. Some local Persian garrisons resisted, but without coordinated leadership, they could not fend off the Arabs' unified tactics. The notion of a desert force challenging the grand empire might have seemed improbable a generation earlier, yet now the Arab armies advanced steadily, emboldened by each small victory.

Sasanian nobles disagreed on how to respond. Some believed they could crush the Arab threat if they only stabilized the monarchy, calling for a single king to unify the country. Others viewed the Arabs as less dangerous than internal rivals; they delayed or withheld troops, hoping to maintain power in their own districts. These divisions prevented a decisive counterstrike and allowed the Arabs to gain strong footholds, particularly in the region near the Euphrates, which provided an entry point into the heartland of Mesopotamia.

Early Confrontations: Qadisiyyah and Beyond

Several skirmishes preceded the more famous battles, but the confrontation at Qadisiyyah, around 636 CE, stands out. Arab forces, led by skilled commanders loyal to the Rashidun Caliphate, faced a larger but disorganized Persian army under a general named Rostam Farrokhzad. Tradition says that Rostam had difficulty rallying the Sasanian cavalry and coordinating various troops, many of whom were uncertain about the legitimacy of the central government. During the battle, the Arab fighters exploited Sasanian confusion, employing mobile tactics, strong morale, and knowledge gained from prior engagements.

Qadisiyyah lasted several days, featuring violent clashes and episodes of chaos. Accounts speak of dust storms that hindered the heavily armored Sasanian cataphracts, while Arab infantry and cavalry outmaneuvered them. Eventually, Rostam was killed, throwing the Persian ranks into disarray. The defeat opened the route to Ctesiphon, the seat of imperial power. Desperate attempts to muster a second line of defense failed, as noble families bickered about who should command and the empire's figurehead rulers lacked the authority to unify the armies.

When Arab forces marched on Ctesiphon, they found the city ill-prepared for a siege. The Persian court had already fled, taking what remained of the treasury. In 637 CE, the Arabs entered the capital with little resistance, seizing valuable plunder and capturing bureaucratic records. The once-magnificent city that had stood as a symbol of Sasanian grandeur fell almost without a major fight, revealing just how complete the empire's internal collapse was.

Yazdegerd III's Struggle

Although the Arabs took Ctesiphon, the Sasanian Empire did not vanish immediately. Some loyalists rallied behind Yazdegerd III, a young monarch proclaimed as the rightful heir. He tried to gather support among local governors in eastern provinces like Media, Parthia, and Khorasan, hoping that distance from the Arab advance might buy time to rebuild an army.

At first, Yazdegerd found partial success. Certain nobles, alarmed by the conquests in Mesopotamia, recognized that survival depended on uniting under the last legitimate Sasanian prince. They mustered forces in the plateau regions, fortifying some cities. But Yazdegerd had limited funds, no secure central base, and minimal trust among powerful families who had grown accustomed to ignoring the throne's commands. Within a year or two, the Arab armies pressed further east, defeating scattered Sasanian defenders in a series of smaller battles.

The decisive blow came at Nahavand in 642 CE, often called the "Victory of Victories" by Arab chronicles. The remaining Persian forces made a stand, but the result was another rout. Many Sasanian nobles were killed or surrendered. Yazdegerd III retreated further east, wandering among local rulers who offered lukewarm hospitality. He attempted to raise new levies, but the empire's central institutions were gone, and few peasants or provincial lords wanted to continue a losing cause. By 651 CE, Yazdegerd III was reportedly killed by a local miller or guard near Merv, possibly at the instigation of local powers seeking favor with the Arabs. This event marked the symbolic end of the Sasanian dynasty.

Provincial Adaptations and Resilience

Not all regions fell instantly under Arab control. Some remote provinces and mountainous areas resisted for years, forging temporary alliances with local warlords. In parts of the Zagros Mountains or along the Caspian Sea, communities maintained a degree of autonomy, occasionally rebelling against Arab governors. Yet no serious candidate for the Sasanian throne emerged to unify these pockets of resistance into a broader movement.

Meanwhile, Arab administrators sought to incorporate conquered lands into the Caliphate's evolving structure. They allowed many local Persian notables to keep their estates if they agreed to pay taxes and abide by new Islamic governance. Over time, a new class of Persian bureaucrats adapted the old Sasanian administrative systems to serve the Arab governors, ensuring a measure of continuity in record-keeping and taxation. Zoroastrian priests lost their official dominance, but some communities carried on their religious practices under a system of dhimmi status, which required them to pay special taxes for non-Muslims.

Though the official monarchy was gone, Persian cultural life did not cease. Families that once served the court now served the Arab governors, transferring knowledge of governance, irrigation, and city management. Craftsmen continued producing silverware, textiles, and ceramics, though with new motifs reflecting Islamic influences. Over the following centuries, elements of the Sasanian heritage blended with Arab-Islamic culture, contributing to what later became the flourishing of Islamic civilization in Persia.

The Impact on Religion and Society

The fall of the Sasanian state changed the status of Zoroastrianism from a dominant state religion to one of several minority faiths under the Caliphate. Though the new rulers allowed some degree of religious practice, many Zoroastrians eventually converted to Islam for economic or social reasons. Over time, a diaspora of Zoroastrians migrated to places like India (becoming the Parsis), while those who remained in Iran adapted to life under Islamic rule.

For the wider Iranian population, the conquest introduced Arabic language and Islamic law, but it also opened pathways for Persians to rise in the Caliphate's administration. Many Persians embraced Islam sincerely, some intermarried with Arab families, and a fresh Persian-Islamic cultural identity emerged. Classical Persian eventually reasserted itself as a literary language, enriched by Arabic vocabulary, giving rise to new forms of poetry and prose that combined pre-Islamic Iranian traditions with Islamic values.

In the immediate decades after the conquest, daily life for commoners continued much as before in terms of farming and local trade. Over time, taxes were restructured under the Caliphate to align with Islamic principles, and the local aristocracy gradually integrated into the new system, often negotiating to keep their lands. Although the conquests were swift, the deeper process of cultural fusion took generations, eventually producing the distinctive Persianate civilization that blossomed under later Islamic dynasties.

Why Did the Sasanians Collapse So Quickly?

From a long historical perspective, it may seem extraordinary that an empire as old and sophisticated as the Sasanian state could disintegrate within two decades. Several factors help explain the rapid unraveling:

First, the Sasanian monarchy's legitimacy was eroded by internal court intrigues. After Khosrow II, no ruler held the loyalty of all major noble houses. Constant coups and assassinations left the government paralyzed. When faced with a new external threat, the empire could not mobilize effectively or unify its command structure.

Second, the prolonged war with Byzantium had inflicted severe damage on farmland, irrigation networks, and trade routes. Exhaustion and high taxation made peasants less willing to fight or fund further conflict. Wealthy aristocrats were likewise drained of resources and had little appetite for raising fresh armies under uncertain leadership.

Third, the Arab armies arrived with a sense of purpose and unity that contrasted sharply with Persian internal discord. Their commanders had a clear chain of command under the Caliphate, while the Sasanians had no central figure truly capable of rallying national resistance. In some areas, local populations viewed Arab rule as preferable to the extortions of a failing monarchy or indifferent nobles.

Lastly, the ideological appeal of Islam played a role. Many communities, seeing the disarray of Zoroastrian officialdom, found Islam's message of social equality and monotheism compelling. This does not mean mass conversions occurred overnight, but it did help the new rulers establish stable governance, as discontented lower classes sometimes found an opportunity for social advancement under the Caliphate.

The Final Acts of Resistance

Even as Yazdegerd III perished in the east, small pockets of Persian rebels or die-hard Sasanian loyalists carried on token resistance.

Some turned to banditry, raiding Arab-controlled towns. Others tried to form alliances with steppe tribes, hoping to retake major cities. But none of these movements gained enough traction or organization to threaten the Caliphate's hold on the core Sasanian territories.

By the mid to late seventh century, Arab governors oversaw most of what had been the Sasanian realm. In the eighth century, the Abbasid Revolution (750 CE) shifted power from the Umayyad Caliphs in Damascus to the Abbasid Caliphs in Baghdad, a new city founded not far from the old Sasanian capitals. Persian administrators, scholars, and artisans played a significant role in building the Abbasid state, indicating how quickly the talents of the old empire were absorbed into the new order. While some noble houses vanished, others reinvented themselves as part of the Islamic elite, preserving a measure of cultural memory from the Sasanian age.

CHAPTER 20

THE LEGACY OF ANCIENT PERSIA

Introduction

Over these twenty chapters, we have journeyed from the earliest tribes on the Iranian Plateau through the rise and fall of three remarkable empires: the Achaemenids, the Parthians, and the Sasanians. Each dynasty built on the traditions of the one before it, yet each also faced unique challenges that led to its ultimate decline. In this final chapter, we reflect on the enduring legacy of ancient Persia. We will examine how Persian administrative systems, cultural expressions, religious ideas, and conceptions of kingship spread far beyond their original borders. We will also see how, after the Sasanian collapse, the spirit of Iranian identity remained strong and continued evolving under new rulers, including the early Islamic caliphates and later independent Persian dynasties. By understanding these lasting influences, we appreciate the full scope of Persia's contributions to world civilization.

A Bridge Across Dynasties

From the moment Cyrus the Great united the Medes and Persians in the sixth century BCE, Persia established a reputation for effective governance and respect for local customs. The Achaemenids introduced a system of satrapies, roads, and a degree of cultural tolerance that was quite advanced for the time. Although Alexander the Great toppled the Achaemenid Empire, he admired its administrative methods, adopting many Persian officials into his own structure. The Seleucids that followed tried to maintain certain Achaemenid practices, although they never achieved the same unity.

The Parthians, emerging from the northeast, bridged Greek customs with Iranian traditions, forging an empire that lasted centuries despite its loose confederation of noble families. Their mastery of cavalry warfare and willingness to adopt Hellenistic city life made them formidable rivals to Rome. Even though the Parthians eventually succumbed to internal power struggles and the rise of the Sasanians, their imprint on cultural fusion lingered.

When the Sasanians overthrew the Parthians, they revived and expanded the notion of a unified Persian monarchy, blending old Achaemenid symbolism with new administrative refinements. By aligning themselves closely with Zoroastrianism, they forged a state religion that shaped social norms and laws. They continued the Parthian legacy of horse archers and heavy cavalry, while their elaborate court etiquette and architecture built upon older Iranian styles. These dynastic links show how ancient Persia evolved over a thousand years, each empire adding layers of complexity and innovation.

Administrative and Bureaucratic Heritage

One of ancient Persia's most significant contributions lies in the realm of governance. The Achaemenid Empire demonstrated how a vast, multiethnic territory could be administered through local satraps under a central royal authority. This approach influenced subsequent empires, including the Seleucids, Parthians, and Sasanians, all of whom recognized the need for local autonomy balanced by a strong king at the top.

Even after the Arab conquest toppled the Sasanians, many Persian scribes, secretaries, and tax officials continued to serve under the Caliphate. They adapted the old bureaucratic traditions to the new Islamic context, helping the Umayyads and Abbasids manage their realms. Techniques for record-keeping, land surveys, and coin minting all drew from Persian precedents. Over time, these methods spread throughout the Islamic world, blending with Byzantine and other influences to produce a robust administrative culture. Thus, well after the monarchy and fire temples lost their official dominance, the inherited Persian sense of orderly governance remained alive in new forms.

Cultural and Artistic Influence

Ancient Persia also left a profound artistic footprint. The Achaemenid palaces at Pasargadae and Persepolis introduced monumental stone reliefs, columned halls, and grand staircases depicting tribute bearers from many nations. The Parthians contributed a more blended style, merging Iranian dress and motifs with Hellenistic realism. The Sasanians revived and elaborated on rock reliefs, showing kings receiving the divine ring of power or triumphing over Roman emperors. They also excelled in metalwork, producing fine silver plates with hunting scenes and royal feasts.

These artistic traditions did not simply vanish after the Islamic conquests. In the early Abbasid period, Persian artisans in cities like Baghdad and Samarra continued to employ Sasanian techniques for stucco decoration, calligraphy, and architectural design. The idea of an iwan, a vaulted hall open on one side, became a hallmark of Islamic architecture, seen in mosques, palaces, and caravanserais. Persian textile patterns, especially those featuring hunting or floral designs, persisted in weaving traditions that spread across the Middle East and into Europe. The interplay between pre-Islamic and Islamic styles gave rise to a unique Persianate aesthetic that influenced everything from tilework to manuscript illumination.

Religious and Philosophical Currents

The imperial faiths of ancient Persia also shaped religious landscapes far beyond their original scope. Zoroastrianism, codified more fully under the Sasanians, provided deep ethical and cosmological themes that resonated even after its loss of official status. Concepts such as the eternal struggle between good (Ahura Mazda) and evil (Ahriman) influenced not just Iranian thought, but also Manichaeism and, to some extent, later religious debates under Islamic rule. Manichaeism, founded by Mani during the Sasanian era, spread across Asia, merging ideas from Christianity, Buddhism, and Zoroastrianism. Though eventually persecuted in Persia, it left a legacy in Central Asia and China.

Ancient Persian tolerance, seen under Cyrus the Great and at times under the Parthians and Sasanians, paved the way for a society where multiple faiths coexisted—though the degree of acceptance varied over time. Even under strict orthodox policies, local communities found ways to practice minority religions. When Islam arrived, it encountered a region already familiar with inter-religious dialogue and state-backed orthodoxy, shaping how conversions occurred and how non-Muslims were integrated. Philosophical questions about free will, the nature of evil, and cosmic dualism found echoes in the theological discussions of Islamic scholars, who sometimes referenced Zoroastrian or Manichaean ideas, even if to refute them.

The Idea of Kingship

Another lasting element of ancient Persia is the concept of the "King of Kings." The Achaemenids were the first to claim that title over a massive territory, symbolizing not just military conquest but moral stewardship over multiple peoples. The Parthians inherited this rhetoric, often styling themselves as successors to earlier Iranian kings, and the Sasanians solidified it by combining monarchy with divine backing from Ahura Mazda.

Though the monarchy ended with the Arab conquests, the image of a just and powerful sovereign lingered in Persian cultural memory. Poets and historians in later Islamic eras, especially during the time of the Persian dynasties like the Samanids, Buyids, and Safavids, drew on Sasanian legends to legitimize their own rule. The epic Shahnameh by Ferdowsi, compiled in the late tenth and early eleventh centuries, retold the grand saga of Persian kings from mythical times to the fall of the Sasanians, preserving the aura of Iranian kingship. This epic helped shape an identity that bridged pre-Islamic and Islamic periods, affirming that Persian culture was continuous despite religious and political upheavals.

Scholarly Transmission and Learning

The transmission of knowledge was another hallmark of Persian influence. In the Achaemenid period, Aramaic scripts facilitated administrative records across the empire. Under the Parthians, Greek learning mingled with Iranian traditions in cities like Seleucia and Ctesiphon. The Sasanians, particularly under Khosrow I, encouraged translations of Greek philosophical and scientific works into Middle Persian, and they welcomed scholars fleeing religious crackdowns in the Byzantine lands. Centers like Gundeshapur became vibrant, hosting a blend of Greek, Indian, and Persian scholarship in fields such as medicine and astronomy.

With the advent of Islamic rule, these traditions continued and even expanded under the Abbasid Caliphate. Persian scholars, many from families that once served the Sasanians, rose to prominence in Baghdad's House of Wisdom. They preserved and enhanced texts from the Greek and Persian past, laying foundations for what is often called the Islamic Golden Age of science and philosophy. Indeed, the synergy between Arabic as a language of religion and administration and the Persian legacy of scholarship proved immensely fruitful, guiding intellectual pursuits across the Middle East for centuries.

National Identity and Cultural Pride

The collapse of the Sasanian Empire did not erase a sense of Iranian identity. Over time, Iranians embraced Islam yet maintained a distinct cultural heritage. The Persian language survived and eventually flourished as a literary and courtly medium, especially under the Samanids in eastern Iran. Writers and poets celebrated pre-Islamic stories and heroes, weaving them into the Islamic context. From the tenth century onward, a renewed sense of Iranian pride emerged, symbolized by the completion of the Shahnameh, which recounted the entire history of Persian kings from mythic beginnings to Yazdegerd III's fall.

This blending of pre-Islamic and Islamic layers forged a resilient Iranian identity. Dynasties like the Buyids, who were Shi'a and recognized the Abbasid Caliph's spiritual authority but effectively ruled their own states, consciously invoked Sasanian-like titles. They revived certain court rituals and minted coins reflecting a fusion of old and new. Later, under the Safavids (1501–1736 CE), a distinctly Iranian Shi'a state took shape, once again drawing on the memory of ancient Persia to reinforce legitimacy. Even if the monarchy no longer claimed to be a direct continuation of the Achaemenid or Sasanian line, the cultural echoes were unmistakable.

Global Influence Beyond the Middle East

Persia's influence reached beyond its immediate neighbors. In the ancient world, Achaemenid art and architecture attracted the notice of Greek observers, some of whom admired its elegance while others viewed it as a symbol of tyranny. Alexander's own empire-building approach was shaped by Persian precedents of local autonomy. Later, under the Romans and Byzantines, eastern provinces continued to reflect Persian tastes in luxury goods and court ceremonials. Parthian cavalry tactics impacted Roman military reforms, showing how cross-cultural borrowing influenced the balance of power.

During the medieval period, Sasanian models of governance and courtly etiquette filtered into Islamic courts in North Africa and Spain. As Europeans began to trade more extensively with the Middle East, they encountered Persian textiles, metalwork, and pottery, influencing medieval European art. In China, some lines of Manichaeism and Nestorian Christianity traced their roots back to

Persian missions under the Parthians or Sasanians. Meanwhile, the Silk Road facilitated a broad exchange of ideas and goods, with Persian merchants and envoys leaving impressions on Central and East Asian states.

In modern times, romantic notions of Persia—often conflating Achaemenid, Parthian, and Sasanian images—have inspired scholars, archaeologists, and the general public in the West. Dramatic ruins, such as Persepolis, and epic tales, like those found in the Shahnameh, continue to capture imaginations worldwide, testifying to an enduring global fascination with ancient Persia's grandeur and innovation.

The Enduring Lessons of Ancient Persia

When we consider the overall legacy of the Achaemenids, Parthians, and Sasanians, certain lessons stand out. The notion of effective imperial administration, allowing local populations some autonomy while maintaining central oversight, remains a model studied by historians and political scientists. Cultural tolerance in the Achaemenid realm still resonates as an example of how empires can integrate diverse regions without erasing local identities. The Parthian skill in cavalry warfare reminds us that even a formidable empire like Rome faced limits against flexible and well-trained opponents. The Sasanian combination of state religion and monarchy highlights both the cohesion it can bring and the potential for internal strife when orthodoxy becomes rigid.

Above all, ancient Persia's story is one of adaptation. Each dynasty emerged, succeeded, and fell amid changing circumstances. The Iranian Plateau's challenging environment required robust infrastructure and layered political solutions. Whether forging alliances, co-opting Greek administrators, or adapting siege engines from the Romans, Persian rulers generally embraced innovation. Their downfall typically arrived when their systems ossified, failing to adjust to new threats or social changes. The repeated cycle—strength through adaptation, decline through stagnation—underscores a universal pattern in world history.

Conclusion of Chapter 20

The story of ancient Persia is one of remarkable creativity, administrative prowess, and cultural resilience. From Cyrus the Great's unification of diverse peoples to the final stand of Yazdegerd

III against the Arab armies, the Persians demonstrated how an empire could govern vast territories, blend multiple cultural influences, and cultivate a sense of overarching identity. The legacies of the Achaemenids, Parthians, and Sasanians did not simply vanish after military defeat. Their influence endured in administrative structures, religious thought, courtly ceremonies, and the enduring mythos of Iranian kingship.

Under subsequent Islamic rule, Persian language, art, and scholarship contributed profoundly to the broader Muslim world. Indeed, the medieval Islamic civilizations that rose in Baghdad, Nishapur, and beyond owe a significant debt to the administrative genius and cultural sophistication passed down through centuries of Persian statecraft. Even in modern Iran, echoes of ancient Persia linger in language, literary traditions, festivals, and a persistent pride in a heritage that spans millennia.

With the end of this chapter, we conclude our exploration of the complete history of the Persian Empire, from its prehistoric foundations to the final days of the Sasanian dynasty. Though these empires rose and fell, each left indelible marks on human civilization, reminding us of the power of governance, art, religion, and adaptable leadership to shape the destiny of nations. May their stories continue to inspire study, reflection, and wonder in generations to come.

Help Us Share Your Thoughts!

Dear reader,

Thank you for spending your time with this book. We hope it brought you enjoyment and a few new ideas to think about. If there was anything that didn't work for you, or if you have suggestions on how we can improve, please let us know at **kontakt@skriuwer.com**. Your feedback means a lot to us and helps us make our books even better.

If you enjoyed this book, we would be very grateful if you left a review on the site where you purchased it. Your review not only helps other readers find our books, but also encourages us to keep creating more stories and materials that you'll love.

By choosing Skriuwer, you're also supporting **Frisian**—a minority language mainly spoken in the northern Netherlands. Although **Frisian** has a rich history, the number of speakers is shrinking, and it's at risk of dying out. Your purchase helps fund resources to preserve and promote this language, such as educational programs and learning tools. If you'd like to learn more about Frisian or even start learning it yourself, please visit **www.learnfrisian.com**.

Thank you for being part of our community. We look forward to sharing more books with you in the future.

Warm regards,
The Skriuwer Team

www.ingramcontent.com/pod-product-compliance
Lightning Source LLC
LaVergne TN
LVHW012044070526
838202LV00056B/5584